KUGEL,

KNISHES,

AND

OTHER TASTY

DISHES

KUGEL,
KNISHES,
AND
OTHER TASTY
DISHES

A collection of 280 traditional Jewish
recipes for holidays and anytime.
125 are for kugel.

Nina Yellin

Smylan Reed Books

Edited by Michael Blasenheim, Faye Lepp, and Marla Stafford
Illustrations by Nina Yellin
Kugel Song by Nina Yellin, arranged by Melody Blasenheim
Latke Song by Debbie Friedman

Other books by Nina Yellin:

The Kugel Book Featuring Madame á la Kugel, 1988
The Kugel Story, Not Just Noodle Pudding, 1991
The Kugel Story, Not Just Noodle Pudding 2, 1993
Hagadah for the Next Generation, 2001

Printed in the U.S.A.

Smylan Reed Books
P.O. Box 271314
Flower Mound, TX 75027-1314
972-317-3220 smylan@airmail.net

LCCN: 00-092702
ISBN 0-9622811-2-3

First Edition

All standard measurements in this book are American.
All temperatures are Fahrenheit.

Glossary in the back of book explains
terms you may not recognize.

DEDICATED

To Melody, Mike, Lisa, Bill, Daniel, Steve, and Bubbie

ABOUT THE COVER

Stretch your imagination!

The Hebrew letters "hay" and "yud" spell the word "chai" which means "life." Kugel, knishes, and other tasty dishes that appear in this book can of course, when used in moderation, sustain life. Therefore "chai" very abstractly appears on the cover.

The ribbony shapes of the "hay" and ribbon at the bottom of the design double as giant noodles, the one ingredient most used in the preparation of kugel. A rectangle is the most common shaped pan used for baking it.

On the left side of letter, "hay" is a special "noodle" which triples as a twisted Havdalah candle, and the "yud" doubles as a flame. The Havdalah candle is used Saturday night at the closing Sabbath service. Kugel, knishes, and my other tasty dishes are frequently served before and during the Sabbath, and at holiday and ceremonial meals.

BUNDLES OF THANKS

Thanks to the following people for the time they spent looking things over and for their suggestions: Rabbi Geoffrey Dennis, Michael Blasenheim, Marla Stafford, Faye Lepp, Ricki Deragisch, Ellen Tillotson, Suzanne Byron, Katherine Dulle and Betty Dunn.

Thanks for computer technical support: Bill Jackson, Gwen and Steve Lewis.

Thanks to the recipe testers: Cheryl Szuch, Diane Seligmann, Linda Tavano, Judith Bernstein, Lynne Pewterbaugh, Sue Byron, Joanne Moss, Betty Dunn, Faye Lepp, Suzie Fintz, Connie Kruger, Judy Feldman, Melody Blasenheim, and Lisa Schlichtig.

Thanks to everyone below who contributed recipes: Betty Field, Myrna Cohen, Paula Costanzo, Diane Winstin, Jerry Yellin, Merle Pollack, Diane Dubin, Mel Silverman, Laurie Zelnick, Bobbi Barr, Chris Thomas, Cecile Alexander, Vivian Friedman, Sheila Goodman, Nancy Deutsch, David Deutsch, Mae Rosenthal, Barbara Telanoff, Marilyn Moskowitz, Betty Schwartz, Claire Yellin, Cindy Yellin, Gertrude Schaffer, Eileen Rosen, Barbara Polonsky, Nadine Friedman, Elaine Gross, Judy Stern, Merle Rotman, Lee Sitron, Pearl Alcoff, Jo Urbanelli, Morna Traffas, Barbara Haber, Sophie Marcus Treibwasser, Mort Lynn, Deen Kogan, Shari Donahue, Lynne Moyle, Cookie Shifris, Ricki Deragisch, Marianne Cagle, Celia Elner, Amy Cherrnay, Joanne Moss, Heidi Whitaker, Hilda Golden, Eileen Redwood, Barbie Kemerer, and Dorie Sand.

Thanks to the music makers: Melody Blasenheim for arranging "The Kugel Song" and to Debbie Friedman for permission to use "The Latke Song."

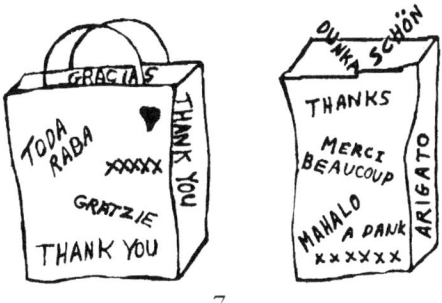

7

TABLE OF CONTENTS

Yellin Family Kugel, Vegetable Knishes, and Latkes

PREFACE

<u>Kugel, Knishes, and Other Tasty Dishes</u> features the most popular dishes in primarily Ashkenazic (Central and Eastern European) Jewish cooking. They are the foods that I grew up with. Other Jewish recipes that appear are Middle Eastern and Sephardic (with Spanish ancestry).

Kugel and knishes appear on menus in just about every Jewish delicatessen in America. Knishes are sold from carts by some vendors on street corners in New York City. One or the other will be, more often than not, served as a side dish at parties and celebrations. Miniature knishes are often included as hors d'oeuvres and a sweet kugel will sometimes appear for dessert. Although there are many varieties of knishes, kugels are far more diverse. My ingredient shopping list is almost endless.

In my family — since I was knee high to a grasshopper — a simcha or holiday meal was not complete without kugel. Until I was an adult, I did not know that a bagel and lox meal could be ingested without a savory piece. Sweet Cherry Kugel was my mother's favorite to serve with a dairy meal and potato kugel was usually part of the Friday night dinner. Sometimes a sweet or not sweet pareve noodle kugel was served in its place. At the Passover Seder, the whole family looked forward to eating Aunt Myrna's Apple, Nut, and Raisin Matzo Kugel.

People have asked what ever possessed me to write kugel cookbooks. In 1988 I had a Hanukkah party and asked three of my cousins to bake kugel. Each of their recipes was different than any that I had in my limited collection at that time. I wondered how many more recipes there were in the world for this wonderful treat, and asked all of my friends and relatives

13

for recipes. I also became curious about history and pronunciation differences so while waiting for recipes, I did extensive kugel research.

Several months after my query, I had in my collection more than 200 kugel recipes, which I narrowed down to 175. Since the publication of my early books, due to similarities, and those I felt were not very good, I cut back the number of kugel recipes to 125.

This book answers the original five questions:

What is a kugel? Where does it come from?
How do you say it? When do you eat it? Why?

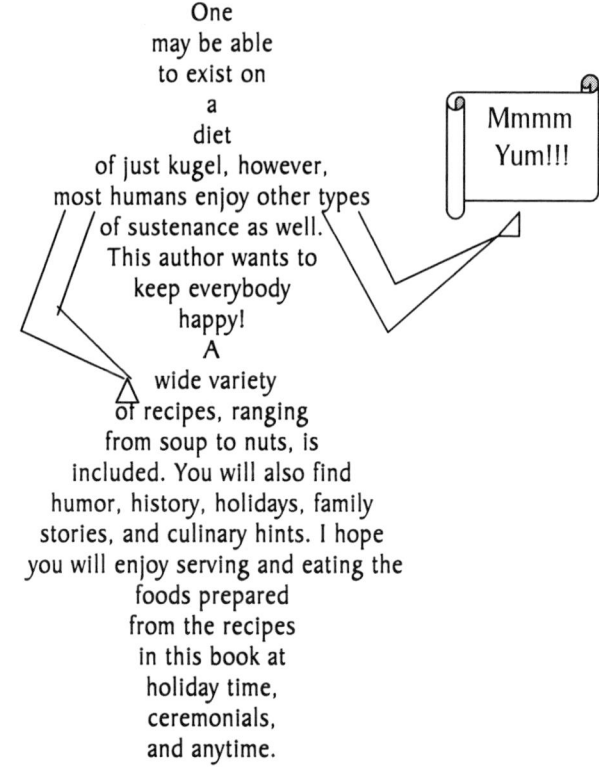

One
may be able
to exist on
a
diet
of just kugel, however,
most humans enjoy other types
of sustenance as well.
This author wants to
keep everybody
happy!
A
wide variety
of recipes, ranging
from soup to nuts, is
included. You will also find
humor, history, holidays, family
stories, and culinary hints. I hope
you will enjoy serving and eating the
foods prepared
from the recipes
in this book at
holiday time,
ceremonials,
and anytime.

Mmmm
Yum!!!

INTRODUCTION

This is a kosher cookbook.

KOSHER CLASSIFICATIONS

Recipes that are suitable for the following types of meals are designated:

(M) *Milchig* or dairy (F) *Fleishig* or meat
(P) *Pareve* or neutral (foods that can be served with any meal).

Recipes designated (T) are "treife" or unfit — they are not kosher. This is primarily a kosher cookbook; however, for historic or humorous interest, a few treife recipes appear.

BEING KOSHER

Judaism is an all-encompassing way of life. It is a culture that includes religion, song, dance, art, language, and food. The laws of kashruth, which are primarily food-related, apply to all daily requirements of Jewish ritual life. The observance goes beyond what I have written.

Dietary laws of kashruth are taken from the Bible's Five Books of Moses and have been followed for thousands of years. Kosher or *"kasher"* in Hebrew means "fit" or "proper." Any health value is considered coincidental.

15

To prepare a strictly kosher recipe, packaged ingredients must be certified through rabbinical supervision. There are several kosher certification organizations in the United States and each has its own symbol. Labels on packaged grocery products that have been certified are marked with either a "K" for *"kosher"* or a "U." The "U" within a circle is the symbol of the Orthodox Union (the largest kosher certification organization in the United States). If you will be preparing a pareve recipe, also look for a "P" on the packaging.

Fresh kosher meat and poultry are sold at kosher butcher shops. Frozen kosher meat and poultry can be found in many grocery stores in freezer-cases that are used only for kosher foods.

In order to allow food to digest after eating a meat meal, it is customary to wait for six hours before consuming a dairy meal. However, it is permissible to eat a dairy meal one-hour after eating meat, as long as something pareve has been eaten after the dairy food. The mouth must also first be thoroughly rinsed or a drink must be consumed. In addition, one must also wash his or her hands. For people with special dietary needs and for children under the age of nine, allowances can be made and a rabbi should be consulted.

In the kitchen, two separate sets of dishes, pots and pans, silverware and utensils are kept for dairy and meat meals. Some people use just use one set of glass dishes. They are pareve and can be used with any meal. Because glass can be seen through, it is said that it can be cleaned more thoroughly than china, plastic, or porcelain. Paper plates and cups and plastic utensils are also permitted.

To make the kitchen kosher for the holiday of Passover, kitchenware used at other times during the year are stored away and two other sets are used. Processed foods must be approved for this holiday. For more about kashruth and Passover see the Passover Kugel section of this book (p. 114).

FOODS THAT ARE PERMITTED

1. Pareve Products — Foods that can be eaten in their natural state, such as fruits, vegetables, nuts, grains, eggs, fish, etc. are *"pareve"* (pronounced par-reh-vuh or par-vuh), meaning "neutral." They can therefore be eaten with dairy or meat meals.

2. Dairy Products — These products, and meals prepared with dairy products are called *"milchig"* (pronounced mil-hig), meaning "milk." The word denotes dairy foods, dishes, and utensils.

Dairy substitutes can be used in a pareve meal as long as they are certified kosher and pareve. The federal government allows sodium caseinate (considered to be dairy) in what are called "non-dairy" powders. "Coffee Mate" is not pareve for this reason.

3. Meat and poultry — Meats must be from only peaceful, cloven- or split-hoofed animals who graze and chew their cud such as cows, sheep, goats, and deer. Some parts are not kosher. Poultry must be barnyard birds, such as chickens, ducks, turkeys, and geese. Birds and animals must be killed quickly and painlessly under religious supervision. They must be thoroughly bled (since the consumption of blood is strictly forbidden). They must also be salted, soaked, and inspected for kosher certification. Liver, which does not need to be soaked and salted, must be broiled. These foods are *"fleishig"* (flay-shig), meaning flesh. The word denotes meat food, dishes, and utensils.

4. Additives, such as gelatin, must come from kosher-certified animals. Lecithin must come from soybeans or eggs, pectin from citrus fruits or apples.

FOODS THAT ARE NOT PERMITTED

1. Pork products, meat from carnivorous animals and birds, shellfish, fish without scales and fins, and almost all crawling and swarming things such as insects, snakes, and reptiles are *"treife"* (tayf), meaning unfit.

2. Dairy products and meat cannot be cooked together nor eaten together in the same meal. Exodus 23:19: "you shall not cook a kid in its mother's milk."

3. Fish, although pareve, should not be eaten together with meat or poultry. It may be eaten either before or after a meat or poultry as long as it is served on a separate plate with separate utensils.

EGGS AND KASHRUTH

Although sold in the dairy section of the grocery store, eggs are not considered, in Jewish law, to be "dairy." They are pareve and can be served and/or cooked with either meat (fleishig) or dairy (milchig) meals.

Since the consumption of blood is strictly forbidden, an egg with a blood spot, which would indicate that the egg was fertilized or diseased, would not be kosher and should be discarded along with any food it touches. To avoid spoiling a recipe, a kosher cook will first check for spots by cracking each egg that is to be used into a cup.

Note: The average hen lays 277 eggs a year or enough so you can make one kugel each week for a year!

18

KUGEL

Sugar and Spice and Everything Nice, that's what kugels are made of.

When times were prosperous fruits, vegetables, sugar and spice were added. Sugar and cinnamon have always been favorite additions to foods. Cinnamon has been used extensively in Jewish cuisine since before King Solomon's time. Trade with spice producing countries in the far east had been an important occupation of the Jews until the 20th century. Jews have always had a passion for sugar. It was brought from Asia to Europe in 636 A.C.E. In the 14th century, Jews introduced sugar to the Western world. Today, as it has been for hundreds of years, cinnamon and sugar are used more often than any other spices in kugels. Cottage cheese has been used in Europe for several hundred years. It is made from skim milk and its benefit as a low calorie substitute for meat was recognized after World War I. It is one of the staple food items of a kugel mavin (as well as sour cream and cream cheese, noodles, butter or margarine and other things).

KUGEL

When some people hear the word "kugel" they shriek and imagine red lights flashing "stop" and flags waving a warning "high fat and cholesterol food." I say, "no, no, no! It is not necessary to feel that way. Kugel can be very nourishing and part of a healthy diet." Fruits or vegetables, dairy products, spices, nuts, and other ingredients are included in hundreds of different combinations to comprise wonderful sweet or not sweet kugels.

The average slice of kugel contains only 1/4 of a whole egg. Egg whites or egg substitutes can be used. See the back of this book for a complete set of substitution lists.

WHAT'S A KUGEL?

Kugel is a light-to-heavy, semi-moist, solid, bread-like pudding or casserole-type food that is very popular in Jewish cuisine and is usually kosher. It is extremely versatile and can be served hot or cold as a main or side dish, for dessert, breakfast, lunch, dinner, or at snack time. This great crowd-pleaser is often served at Jewish holiday and ceremonial meals.

Although bread-like in consistency, kugels are not bread; they are in a class of their own. However, some kugels use bread or bread crumbs as a base. Grains or potatoes are sometimes used as a base, giving kugel a farinaceous or farina-like consistency. The most frequently used starch is the noodle and kugel is often described as "noodle pudding."

Some recipes are gourmet; however, most are very easy to prepare with as few as four ingredients. Many include all four basic food groups. The Kugel Shopping List (p. 32) includes a huge variety of ingredients that are used to prepare these delicious and nutritious crowd pleasers.

Cheese-noodle kugels can be sweet or not sweet. The cheeses used are usually not stringy when melted and are seldom sharp. When legumes (i.e. peas and beans), corn, or tomatoes are used (except for sun-dried), the casserole is not a kugel. If candies (such as chocolate) are included, it would be a cake (or something) but not a kugel! People have asked me if lasagna can be considered a kugel. I say NO. Let kugel be kugel and lasagna be lasagna!

Sweet kugels can be served for morning breakfast, late night breakfast, or to break the fast at sundown Yom Kippur — the Day of Atonement. They can also be eaten at brunch, lunch, snack-time, dinner, or even as dessert. But be careful — it is habit-forming and absolutely irresistible. Beware of leftovers!

Kugels that are not sweet best served as a main course at lunchtime with fruit and salad, or as a side dish at dinner with a meat, poultry, or fish meal.

Kugel derived its name due to its shape, which was usually round in early kugel history. There is a theory that kugel is a traditional holiday food because its shape was like a mound of manna. Manna falls from the tamarisk tree in June and July and provided nourishment for the early Israelites during their journey across the desert when food was scarce. They called it "manna from heaven."

Kugel is either baked in an oven, steamed in the center of a cholent (stew) or cooked stovetop (p. 97) in a heavy iron skillet. Today it is usually baked in a square or rectangular-shaped baking pan — sizes varying from 8" x 8" to 11" x 16" — unless you are a caterer. Then it is HUGE! (See Cool Whip Jygunda Kugel (p. 46). Occasionally kugel will be baked in muffin tins or round pans. I feel that 2 inches high is best, but some people like kugel that is much higher. Servings are usually cut into 2- to 3-inch squares.

There are no set rules as to how or when kugel should be served or eaten. Usually it is eaten with a fork, but if it is cold and solid, it can be eaten with one's fingers — as long as no one is looking!

THE GREAT KUGEL
PRONUNCIATION DEBATE
Kugel, Koogle, or Kigle?

Most people, including me, say *"kugel"* — the "U" is pronounced the same as the "oo" in the word good. This is the *Litvak* (Lithuanian) and Yiddish form of pronunciation. A *Galitzian* or *Galitzianer* (a person from Galicia — an area stretching across southeastern Poland to southwestern Russia, whose borders have changed frequently throughout history) would say *"kigle"* (sounds like wiggle), which is the Hebrew pronunciation. The American/German pronunciation is *"koogle."* The "oo" is pronounced the same as the "oo" in the word "coo," the sound doves and babies make. Cows do it too but they put mmmm in front. "Mmmm" is, of course, the sound people make when they eat kugel.

What it really boils down to is that pronunciation differences occur depending on where one is from, or one's ancestors. According to my friend who grew up in Upper Darby, Pennsylvania, everyone in her neighborhood said "kigle." Another friend told me that when she lived in Chicago everyone also called it "kigle." In fact, when she was growing up, she thought kugel was a sweet kigle, but she had never tasted a sweet kugel until she moved to the east.

Lithuania and Galicia are areas that were very heavily populated by Jews. The Litvak Jews were very influential in their communities and were very much involved in business. It was their Yiddish pronunciation, "kugel," that was considered proper.

The Galitzians were primarily Hassidim or Hassidic. The Hassidim (also spelled C-h-a-s-s-i-d-i-m) are a sect of very pious Orthodox Jews that was formed in 1750 CE. The men, who wear long beards and earlocks, are quite distinctive in their striking black coats and hats. In Galicia, they were a folksy, peasant-type people. A Galitzian might argue that the Hebrew pronunciation "kigle" is the only way to say the word.

Now you may ask the question, "What happens to the pronunciation when one's mother is a Galitzian and one's father is a Litvak?" This happened to my cousin, Paula Costanzo. I think it has something to do with which parent has the dominant pronunciation genes!

Yiddish definition — (kugel) — pudding

Hebrew definition — (kigle) — round

German definition — (koogle) — ball, sphere, globe, cannon.

Many people pronounce "kugel" as "koogle." Kugel's origin is German. However, several years ago I was told by a Jewish woman from Germany that kugel is now non-existent in that country. The closest thing to a kugel in Germany, she said, is *"schalet,"* a baked mixture of bread, potatoes, eggs, salt, and pepper — ingredients used in Pennsylvania Dutch (or PA. German) potato bread stuffing.

Kugels have been in existence since the Middle Ages. In the year 1100 CE, they were described in Germany as bread. The recipes traveled eastward from Germany along with the Ashkenazic Jews and eventually they made their way into Russia, where most kugels are not sweet. The only sweetness would come from the occasional addition of raisins.

Local customs, dietary laws, and lack of money throughout history drastically affected the types of food available to the Jews. Food supplies of the Ashkenazic Jews were often very limited since they lived primarily in cold regions. Vegetables were available only during the harvest season and were not considered very important in most Ashkenazic Jewish homes. In their place, kugels were substituted. Because pepper was a popular spice and "Salt and Pepper Kugels" became a favorite.

The majority of American Jews are Ashkenazic (of central and eastern European descent). So it is their traditions and cuisine that have become the most popular in the USA. Most of the kugels that we are familiar with today are Ashkenazic.

Some Very Old Recipes

ASHKENAZIC SALT AND PEPPER KUGEL (F)

    3 cups broad noodles, cooked and drained
  3/4 cup chicken fat (schmaltz)
    4 eggs, well beaten
      salt and pepper

Preheat oven to 400°.   4 servings.

Add to noodles salt and pepper to taste, eggs and fat. Pour into greased casserole dish. Bake until top is well browned, about 45 minutes.

In the year 1500 CE Polish Jews were making matzo farfel kugels and they were possibly the first made for Passover.

MATZOS PUDDING (F)

3 matzos (soaked, pressed and stirred until smooth),
10 eggs beaten separately,
2 large apples (peeled and grated),
1 cup goose fat,
1/2 cup white wine,
  Grated rind of a lemon,
  Sugar to sweeten,
1/2 teaspoon salt.

Stir one-half hour, and lastly fold in the beaten egg whites. Grease form well, bake in a moderate oven one-half hour, and serve with wine sauce: six eggs, one-cup weak wine, sugar to taste. Stir constantly until it thickens as it is apt to curdle.

Note: Old recipes are written exactly as they originally appeared, including spelling, punctuation, and grammar.

The first kugel recipes to be printed in America were in the Settlement Cookbook, published in 1903 CE by Mrs. Simon Kinder. This book consists primarily of German recipes. It is not a "kosher" cookbook and recipes in it may be treife. The book was written to raise money for the poor, newly arrived Russian immigrants. The following recipes are from the Settlement Cookbook.

NOODLE PUDDING (M)

1 pint milk
2 ounces butter, heated

In this boil some fine noodles and cool, add five yolks of eggs, beaten, with five tablespoonfuls sugar, one pint sour cream, five egg whites, beaten stiff. Bake and serve with wine sauce: six eggs, one cup weak wine, sugar to taste. Stir constantly until it thickens.

KUGEL (T)

Soak five wheat rolls in water, then press the bread quite dry. Knead it with three-fourths pound raw suet,* two heaping handfuls brown sugar, one tablespoonful molasses, cinnamon, cloves and lemon, one tablespoonful water, a pinch of salt. Mix very well together. Line an iron pot with alternate layers of above dough and stewed and stoned prunes. Bake two hours; baste often with prune juice.

VIENNESE NOODLE PUDDING (M)

8 ounces noodles
1-1/4 cups milk
3 eggs, separated
2 teaspoons plus 3 tablespoons butter
Salt and pepper, to taste

Preheat oven to 350°.   6 servings.

Break noodles into small pieces and cook in milk until well done. Let them cool but do not drain. Grease an 8- or 9-inch frying pan (with metal handle so it will not melt in oven) with the 2 teaspoons butter. Cream the remaining butter. Add the yolks one by one, beating steadily. Add the noodles with the milk. Beat egg whites until stiff but not dry and fold into noodles. Season with salt and pepper to taste. Spread mixture evenly in the greased pan and bake 40 to 50 minutes or until lightly browned. Cool slightly. Loosen edges and turn out onto a warm plate.

The Jewish Manual, printed in 1846 and edited anonymously by "A Lady," was the first Jewish cookbook printed in English. It contains some of the earliest kugel recipes. Kugel and Commean is a recipe for a cholent, or stew, baked in a basin (or large pot) with a kugel. It calls for Spanish peas (garbanzos or chick peas), beans, and all-night baking in a baker's oven, possibly serving it with lemon and brandy sauce.

Shred suet may not be kosher, and therefore, the next recipe is possibly treife. The portion of the recipe in [] brackets is the kugel, referred to later in the recipe as pudding.

KUGEL AND COMMEAN (F OR T)

Soak one pint of Spanish peas and one pint of Spanish beans all night in three pints of water; take two marrow bones, a calf's foot, and three pounds of fine gravy-beef, crack the bones and tie them to prevent the marrow escaping, and put all together into a pan; [then take one pound of flour, half a pound of shred suet, a little grated nutmeg and ground ginger, cloves and allspice, one pound of coarse brown sugar, and the crumb of a slice of bread, first soaked in water and pressed dry, mix all these ingredients together into a paste, grease a quart basin and put it in, covering the basin with a plate set in the middle of the pan with the beans, meat, etc.]. Cover the pan lightly down with coarse brown paper, and let it remain all the night and the next day, (until required) in a baker's oven, when done, take out the basin containing the pudding, and skim the fat from the gravy which must be served as soup; the meat, etc., is extremely savory and nutritious, but is not a very seemly dish for table. The pudding must be turned out of the basin, and a sweet sauce flavored with lemon and brandy is a fine addition.

A very popular dessert pudding during the 18th century in Great Britain was called "Vermicelli Pudding." The recipe below was taken from a rare book called The English Art of Cookery, According to Present Practice by Richard Briggs, published in 1788 CE in Dublin. It can be found at the Schlesinger Library of Radcliffe College, Harvard University. Many kugel recipes used today have been adapted from this old favorite.

18TH CENTURY VERMICELLI PUDDING (M)

Take a quarter of a pound of vermicelli, and boil it in a pint of milk till it is tender with a flick of cinnamon and a laurel leaf or two; then take out the cinnamon and laurel leaf, and put in half a pint of cream, a quarter of a pound of butter melted, the same weight of sugar, with the yolks of six eggs well beat; lag a puff-pastre round the edge of your dish, put it in, and bake it three quarters of an hour in a moderate oven. For variety, you may add half a pound of currants clean washed and picked.

Note: Old recipes are written exactly as they originally appeared, including spelling, punctuation, and grammar.

KUGEL SHOPPING LIST

You're gonna bake a kugel? OK Nana Nina. Now I'm ready to shop!

The following list is intended only to point out the extensive variety of ingredients used to make kugels. But fear not! You do not have to have all of these ingredients at your fingertips, to consider yourself a kugel maven (expert)!

BASIC INGREDIENTS FOR MOST POPULAR KUGELS

Vanilla, cinnamon
Eggs or egg whites
Butter or margarine
Sugar — white, granulated
Apples, crushed pineapple
Noodles — fine, medium, wide
Raisins — black or white seedless
Cream cheese, cottage cheese, sour cream

OTHER INGREDIENTS USED

Noodles: Spaghetti, whole wheat, spinach, Passover, no yolk, orzo

Flours: Presifted, unbleached, whole wheat

Breads: Crumbs, loaf breads, rolls, matzo

Cereals: Corn Flakes, Frosted Flakes, farina

Crackers: Graham cracker crumbs

Grains: Bulgur, millet, pearl barley, brown or white rice (not instant), grits, kasha (groats)

Potatoes: White, sweet

Oil: Canola, corn, safflower, olive, peanut, sunflower

Sweeteners: Sugar (brown, white, confectioners), heat-stable artificial sweetener, honey, juices

Cheeses: cheddar, Parmesan, ricotta, farmer, cottage, Muenster

Creams: light, heavy, half and half, pareve non-dairy creamer, whipped topping

Milk: powdered dry, liquid whole, skim

Yogurt: banana, plain, vanilla, raspberry

Spices:	Salt, pepper, paprika, ginger, allspice, nutmeg, cinnamon, cloves, coriander, cumin
Herbs:	Dill, parsley (dry or fresh)
Extracts:	Vanilla, almond, vanilla-butternut, brandy
Baking agents:	Baking powder
Soups:	Broth (chicken), dry soup mix (chicken, onion)
Puddings:	Vanilla, banana
Nuts/Seeds:	Almonds, walnuts, pecans, mixed, sunflower seeds
Vegetables:	Carrots, broccoli, cabbage, spinach, zucchini, mushrooms, celery, red and green bell pepper, cauliflower
Grebenes:	Cracklings
Fish and Meats:	Cooked, smoked or canned fish, liver, chicken

Fruits:	Fresh:	Apples
		Apricots
		Pineapple
		Grapes
		Peaches
		Plums
	Prepared pie filling:	Apples, Cherries Pineapple
	Dried:	Apricots
		Coconut
		Dates
		Prunes
	Canned:	Grapes
		Pineapple
		Oranges
		Peaches
		Fruit Cocktail
	Sauces:	Applesauce
	Juices:	Apple, apricot nectar, lemon, orange
	Peels:	Lemon, orange
	Jams:	Apricot, pineapple, prickly pear

MAKE A PLAIN KUGEL FANCY

Many sweet kugels are delicious when topped with cinnamon, sugar, whipped cream, sour cream, yogurt, or fresh, canned, or prepared fruit. For fancier dessert kugels, use the diagrams below. Use drained crushed, or chunk pineapple, or prepared cherry, apple, or blueberry pie topping. Substitute apple pie filling for crushed pineapple, if desired. Sprinkle slivered almonds over any of the toppings for an added touch.

EASY

Cover kugel with cherries. Scatter pineapple chunks on top or make a design with cherries and crushed pineapple as shown here.

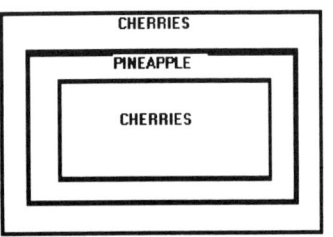

RED, WHITE, AND BLUE

Place blueberries in area for stars. Sprinkle with slivered almonds. Cover the rest of kugel with sour cream. Place pie cherries on top for every other stripe.

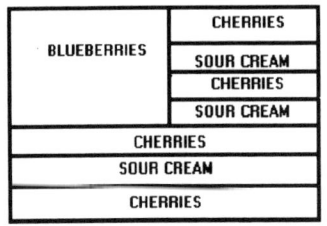

HARLEQUIN

Draw a line down the center of the kugel. Draw two large "X's." Fill with crushed pineapple, pie cherries, and blueberries.

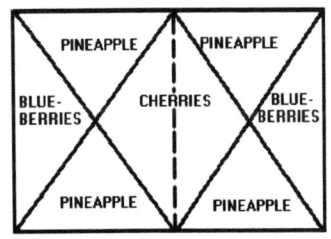

FREEZING A KUGEL

✡ Do not freeze potato kugels because they will be watery when defrosted.

✡ Vegetable kugels, when indicated in recipe, should not be frozen. They will be too watery after defrosting.

✡ Leftovers — wrap tightly in freezer wrap, freezer proof plastic container, or plastic wrap and foil and freeze for up to 4 weeks.

✡ Unbaked kugel — cover mixture with freezer wrap or with plastic wrap and then aluminum foil. Freeze in pan for up to 4 weeks. Thaw overnight and bake according to instructions in recipe.

✡ Baked whole kugel — bake 15 minutes less than recipe calls for. Cool and then cover with freezer wrap or plastic wrap and aluminum foil. Freeze for up to 4 weeks. Place thawed kugel in preheated oven and bake in preheated oven 15 minutes at temperature recommended in recipe.

NOODLE KUGEL

NOODLES

Just about every country in the world has its own form of noodle. Today there are more than 300 different types. However, only a few are used in kugels — primarily fine, medium, broad, and vermicelli noodles. In addition, spinach and whole wheat are sometimes used for a healthier twist. The packaged egg or plain varieties are fine to use, as is no-yolk. If you prefer, use fresh or homemade noodles. The use of shell noodles, elbow macaroni, or bowtie noodles in a kugel will make it too heavy.

NOODLES USED IN KUGELS are usually about 2 inches long, however, I also like to use orzo, spaghetti, or fettuccini.

Thin or fine = 1/16 inch wide   Medium = 1/4 inch wide
Wide = 1/2 inch wide   Broad = 1 inch wide

HOMEMADE NOODLE DOUGH (P)

2 cups flour, unbleached and presifted
2 large eggs, beaten
1/3 cup water
1/2 teaspoon salt
1 teaspoon canola oil

Stir together flour and salt. Make a well in center of the mixture. Combine eggs, water, and oil. Pour into center of well and mix with flour thoroughly. Knead on floured board until dough is smooth and elastic (about 10 minutes). Cover with a towel and let rest for 10 minutes. Divide dough into 4 sections. On floured board, roll dough with floured rolling pin to 1/8 inch thickness and 12 inches square. Let stand for 20 minutes. Cut as desired or process floured, flattened dough through the rollers of a pasta machine at widest setting. Fold dough two or three times, flatten, and put through rollers again. Repeat several times until dough is smooth. Adjust machine to the next setting and put through rollers until smooth. Repeat until you get down to the next to the last setting. Cut dough into desired size noodles.

DAIRY NOODLE KUGEL

The story of Judith is thought to have been an inspiration to the Maccabees, and they started baking cheese-filled foods for Hanukkah. From the cheese latkes, p. 194, cheese kugels were derived. American Jews, since the 1950's, have become especially creative in embellishing their kugels. Dairy noodle kugels are the most popular and they are definitely my personal favorites!

SWEET DAIRY NOODLE KUGEL

LUSCIOUS KUGEL (M)

3/4 pound fine noodles, cooked and drained
  4 eggs, beaten
  1 cup sugar
  1 teaspoon vanilla extract
1/2 pound cream cheese, softened
  1 cup warm milk
  1 cup sour cream
1/4 pound butter or margarine, melted

Preheat oven to 325°.   20 servings.

Combine first four ingredients.

Melt cream cheese in warm milk and add sour cream, then melted margarine.

Combine with noodle mixture and pour into greased 9" x 13" pan. Bake 1 hour. Top will be golden.

YELLIN FAMILY KUGEL (M)

1/2 pound medium noodles, cooked and drained
1/4 pound butter or margarine, melted
  6 eggs, separated
  6 ounces cream cheese, softened
  1 pint creamed cottage cheese
1/4 cup sour cream
1/2 cup sugar

Topping: (optional)

2/3 cup graham cracker crumbs
1/3 cup sugar
1/2 stick butter or margarine, melted and cooled

Preheat oven to 350°.   20 servings.

Mix noodles with margarine.

Cream egg yolks and cream cheese together until fluffy. Mix egg yolk mixture with noodles.

Add cottage cheese, sour cream, and sugar. Continue beating until well combined, scrape sides of bowl often.

Beat egg whites until stiff peaks form. Fold into noodle mixture.

Grease a 9" x 13" baking pan and pour in noodle mixture.

Combine topping ingredients. Crumble mixture evenly on top of noodles. Bake for 1 hour. If top is not crispy enough, bake a little longer. Serve hot.

PROUD COW KUGEL (M)

1/2 pound medium wide noodles, cooked and drained
1/2 pound farmer cheese
1/2 pound cottage cheese
1/2 quart milk
1/2 pint sour cream
1/2 teaspoon salt
1-1/2 teaspoons vanilla extract
1/2 dozen eggs, beaten
1/2 cup sugar
1/2 dozen tablespoons butter or margarine, melted

Topping:

1/2 cup slivered almonds
3/4 cup brown sugar

Preheat oven to 350°.   20 servings.

Blend together farmer cheese, cottage cheese, milk, and sour cream. Add remaining ingredients.

Pour mixture into greased springform pan or 9" x 13" baking pan. Bake 1/2 hour. Remove from oven and sprinkle with topping. Bake another hour. If not firm, bake an additional 10 minutes.

41

SIMPLE DAIRY KUGEL (M)

1 pound medium noodles, cooked and drained
6 eggs, beaten
8 ounces cream cheese, softened
1 pint sour cream
1/2 cup sugar
1 teaspoon vanilla extract

Preheat oven to 350°.   20 servings.

Combine eggs, cream cheese, sour cream, sugar, and vanilla.
Mix thoroughly and add to noodles. Pour into greased 9" x 13"
pan. Sprinkle with cinnamon and sugar. Bake 1 hour.

ANOTHER WAY TO MAKE IT KUGEL (M)

1/2 pound medium curly edge noodles, cooked and drained
  4 eggs, beaten
  1 cup sugar
  1 teaspoon vanilla extract
1/4 pound butter or margarine, melted
 12 ounces farmer cheese or drained large curd cottage cheese
1/2 pound cream cheese, softened
  1 pint sour cream, or 8 ounces light peach yogurt
  1 cup milk

Preheat oven to 450°.   20 servings.

Cream eggs with sugar. Add to noodles with vanilla and
butter.

Combine sour cream, cheeses, and milk. Add to noodle
mixture.

Pour into greased 9" x 13" baking pan. Bake at 450° for 5
minutes. Turn oven to 350° and bake 1 hour.

FROSTED FLAKE TOPPED KUGEL (M)

1 pound medium or wide noodles, cooked and drained
6 eggs, beaten
1 pint sour cream
1 cup sugar
1 teaspoon vanilla extract
1/2 pound butter or margarine, melted; reserve 4 tablespoons
3/4 pound cream cheese, softened
1/3 cup lemon juice (optional)
2 tablespoons grated lemon rind (optional)

Topping:

2 cups Frosted Flakes, crushed*
reserved butter or margarine from above

Preheat oven to 325°.   20 servings.

Beat together eggs and sour cream. Add sugar, vanilla, and butter or margarine. Add mashed cream cheese and beat well.

Spread noodles evenly on the bottom of a greased 9" x 13" pan. Pour egg mixture over noodles.

Mix Frosted Flakes with reserved butter or margarine and sprinkle over kugel.

Cover with foil and refrigerate overnight. Bake 1 hour until set.

*Use Corn Flakes instead of Frosted Flakes and just 1/4 pound of margarine.

VIVIAN'S KUGEL (M)

12 ounces medium or wide egg noodles, cooked and drained
5 eggs, beaten
1/2 pound cream cheese, softened
1/2 pound cottage cheese
1 pint sour cream
8 ounces milk
1/4 pound butter or margarine, melted
1 teaspoon vanilla extract
1 teaspoon salt
1/2 cup sugar

Preheat oven to 350°.   20 servings.

Mix together everything, except for the noodles, with electric mixer for 3 to 5 minutes. Add noodles and pour into greased 9" x 13" pan.

Topping:

1/4 pound butter or margarine, melted
2 cups crushed corn flakes
1/2 cup sugar
1 teaspoon ground cinnamon

Combine topping ingredients and sprinkle over noodle mixture. Bake 1 hour.

CEREMONIALS
AND KUGEL FOR A CROWD

Kugel is absolutely the ultimate crowd-pleaser. While I was growing up, my mother always served it whenever there was a family gathering. Today it is still a family favorite.

Ceremonial gatherings where kugel is served are usually a huge success. Babies are practically weaned on it. After all, it is first introduced into their lives when they are just a few days old, at a baby boy's "Ben Zochor." This is a party held on the first Friday after his birth. Eight days after the little guy is born, there will be a B'rith Millah or Bris, the Rite of Circumcision. The relatives will show up again and kugel will again be a part of the goodies. The baby probably is not in the mood to party at this point and wishes the relatives would all just go away. After a bit of a cry, he quietly drinks his bottle and goes to sleep.

One month later, there is another party and this time he is in the mood! This is the Pidyon-Ha-Ben, the Redemption of the Firstborn Son, a ceremony dating back to the sojourn in Egypt. He takes his first good whiff of kugel and he is a very happy child. He can't wait to sink his gums into it!

In non-orthodox families, a party is also given for a newborn girl child after the Simhat Bat (naming ceremony). If she becomes a Bat Mitzvah, usually at age thirteen, kugel might be served at the celebration after the ceremony which marks her as an adult member of the community. The same is true for a 13 year-old boy at his Bar Mitzvah celebration. Kugel will again, perhaps, be served at their weddings.

Kugel will probably be eaten from time to time throughout their entire lives. When they die, the relatives will, no doubt, be eating it again at the gathering after their funerals.

PLANNING A LARGE PARTY?

Serve Cool Whip Jygunda Kugel or consider using
all of the recipes in this book and serve with the following:

ELEPHANT STEW (T)

1 elephant (medium size)
2 rabbits (optional)
  pepper
  salt

Cut elephant into bite-sized pieces. This should take about
two months. Add enough brown gravy to cover. Cook over
high flame for about four weeks or until tender.

This recipe will serve about 3,800, but if more are expected,
two rabbits may be added. Do this only if absolutely
necessary, as most people do not like hare in their stew.

COOL WHIP JYGUNDA KUGEL (M)

1 pound thin noodles, cooked and drained
3 cups sugar
16 extra large eggs, beaten or 8 whole eggs & 16 whites
1-1/2 tablespoons vanilla extract
3-1/2 pounds cream cheese, 1/2 light and 1/2 regular
3 pounds sour cream, 1/2 light and 1/2 regular
1 pound butter or margarine, 1/2 light and 1/2 regular
12 ounces light Cool Whip
  dash cinnamon

Preheat oven to 350°.   72 servings.

Cream together sugar, eggs, and vanilla. Beat in cream cheese,
butter, and sour cream. Add noodles and toss. Fold in cool
whip.

Pour into three 9" x 13" baking pans sprayed with non-stick
baking spray. Distribute noodles and liquid evenly. Sprinkle
with cinnamon. Bake 1 hour until set.

CREAMY CHIFFON KUGEL (M)

The flavor and texture of this kugel is similar to the Cool Whip Jygunda Kugel but it has just a hint of orange flavor. If you like creamsicles, I think you will enjoy the taste of this one.

1/2	pound fine noodles, cooked and drained
1/2	cup sour cream
1/2	cup plain yogurt
1/2	pound cream cheese, softened
4	tablespoons butter or margarine
5	eggs, beaten
1	cup sugar
1/2	teaspoon rum extract
1/4	teaspoon orange extract
1-1/2	cups milk
1/2	cup orange juice

Preheat oven to 350°.   15 servings.

Beat sour cream, yogurt, cream cheese, and butter with electric beaters or food processor until smooth. Pour into a bowl.

Beat together eggs, sugar, and extracts. Add to sour cream mixture.

Beat together the milk and orange juice. Add to other mixture and combine thoroughly. Add noodles and mix well.

Distribute noodles and liquid evenly in greased 9" x 13" pan plus and bake 1 hour.

PEACH HEALTH FOOD KUGEL (M)

1/2 pound wide noodles, cooked and drained
3 eggs, beaten
1-1/2 cups cottage cheese
3/4 cup yogurt
8 ounces cream cheese, softened
1/2 teaspoon vanilla extract
2 teaspoons ground cinnamon
1/4 cup honey
1/8 teaspoon salt
2 tablespoons melted butter or margarine
3 fresh ripe peaches, sliced

Preheat oven to 375°.   20 servings.

Beat together everything except peaches and noodles. Now stir them in. Spread into greased 9" x 13" baking pan.

Topping:

3 tablespoons butter or margarine, melted
1 cup commercial plain bread crumbs
2 teaspoons ground cinnamon
1/4 cup wheat germ
1/4 cup brown sugar
1/2 20-ounce can sliced canned peaches, drained
    maraschino cherries

Combine butter with bread crumbs, cinnamon, wheat germ, and brown sugar. Spread on top of noodle mixture. Bake 50 minutes. Garnish with peaches and cherries after baking.

FRUIT MEDLEY KUGEL (M)

1 pound wide noodles, cooked and drained
4 large eggs, beaten
1/2 cup sugar
1 6-ounce can crushed pineapple, drained; reserve juice
6 ounces cream cheese, softened
1 teaspoon vanilla extract
1 pint sour cream
8 maraschino cherries, halved
1/2 cup raisins
1 apple, grated
6 pitted prunes, cut up

Preheat oven to 350°.   20 servings.

Soften cream cheese in reserved pineapple juice. Mix together all ingredients. Pour into greased 9" x 13" pan.

Topping:

1/2 cup graham cracker crumbs
2 teaspoons sugar
3 dashes ground cinnamon

Mix together topping ingredients and sprinkle over noodle mixture. Bake 1 hour.

FARMER CHEESE, APPLE, AND CHERRY KUGEL (M)

1/2 pound medium noodles, cooked and drained
1 pound farmer cheese
1/2 pound cream cheese, softened
1/4 pound butter or margarine, softened
1 cup milk
1/2 cup sugar
1 teaspoon vanilla extract
5 large eggs, beaten
2 medium sweet apples, pared and grated
1 20-ounce jar prepared pie cherries

Continued on next page.

Farmer Cheese, Apple, and Cherry Kugel continued.

Preheat oven to 350°.   20 servings.

Beat together cheeses and butter until smooth. Add eggs, milk, sugar, and vanilla. Add noodles and apples.

Pour into greased 9" x 13" pan. Bake 45 minutes. Top with pie cherries and bake for 15 minutes more. Serve with sour cream.

PINEAPPLE PRESERVES KUGEL (M)

1 pound noodles, cooked and drained
1/2 pound butter or margarine, melted
4 tablespoons sour cream
1/2 teaspoon ground cinnamon
1/3 cup sugar
1 11-ounce jar pineapple preserves

Preheat oven to 350°.   20 servings.

Add all of the above ingredients to noodles. Pour into 9" x 13" pan sprayed with non-stick baking spray.

Topping:

2 tablespoons butter or margarine, melted
1/2 cup corn flake crumbs
1/2 cup chopped walnuts
1/4 cup sugar
1 teaspoon ground cinnamon

Combine topping ingredients. Place over noodle mixture.
Bake 1 hour.

ORANGE, PINEAPPLE, AND CHERRY KUGEL (M)

    8 ounces fine noodles, cooked al dente
    8 ounces cream cheese, softened
  1/2 cup sour cream
  1/2 cup butter or margarine, softened
    1 cup sugar
    1 teaspoon vanilla extract
    4 medium eggs
    1 16-ounce can mandarin oranges, in own juice, drained
    1 14-ounce can crushed pineapple, in own juice, drained
    1 16-ounce can sweet pitted cherries, in own juice, drained

Preheat oven to 350°.   20 servings.

Beat together everything except fruit and noodles until
blended. Mix noodles and fruit with a spoon and stir into
cheese mixture. Pour into greased 9" x 13" pan.

Topping:

    1 teaspoon ground cinnamon
    1 teaspoon sugar

Combine cinnamon and sugar and sprinkle over kugel
mixture. Bake 1 hour or until set.

DIANE'S APPLE KUGEL (M)

    1 pound medium noodles, cooked and drained
  1/4 pound butter or margarine, melted
1-1/2 cups sugar
    6 large eggs, beaten
  1/2 cup whole milk
    6 large sweet apples, pared and sliced
      dash ground cinnamon
      pinch salt

Preheat oven to 350°.   20 servings.

Continued on next page.

Diane's Apple Kugel continued.

Add butter to cooked noodles and stir. Add remaining ingredients and mix thoroughly.

Pour into greased 9" x 13" pan. Sprinkle heavily with cinnamon. Cover with foil and bake for 30 minutes. Uncover and bake for 30 more minutes.

KUGEL, KOOGLE, KIGLE (M)

12 ounces medium egg noodles, cooked and drained
 5 large eggs, beaten
 8 ounces cottage cheese
 8 ounces sour cream
 6 ounces cream cheese, softened
1/4 pound butter or margarine, softened
 1 6-ounce can crushed pineapple, in own juice, drained
1/2 cup sugar
 1 teaspoon vanilla extract

Optional: Add any of the following fruits —

 1 11-ounce can mandarin oranges, drained
 2 medium tart apples, pared and sliced
 1 8-ounce can peaches, drained
 2 fresh peaches, peeled and sliced
 1 cup mixed seedless grapes

Or spread on top — crushed pineapple, pie cherries, or blueberries.

Preheat oven to 350°.   20 servings.

Mix in a large bowl all ingredients except toppings. Pour into greased 9" x 13" pan. Bake without toppings for about 1 hour.

If toppings are used, bake 45 minutes, then add topping and bake an additional 15 minutes.

CHERRY KUGEL (M)

1 pound medium noodles, cooked and drained
1/2 cup milk
16 ounces cream cheese, softened
6 large eggs, beaten
1/2 cup sugar
1/2 pint sour cream
1 pint creamed cottage cheese
1 teaspoon vanilla extract
1 20-ounce can cherry pie filling

Preheat oven to 350°.   20 servings.

Melt cream cheese in warm milk.

Add beaten eggs, sugar, sour cream, cottage cheese, and vanilla. Beat until thoroughly combined.

Pour into greased 9" x 13" pan. Bake 40 minutes.

Remove from oven, cool, and add fruit topping. Before serving, return to oven 30 minutes. Serve warm.

MOM FIELD'S CHERRY KUGEL (M)

1/2 pound fine noodles, cooked and drained
10 medium eggs, beaten
1 pint cottage cheese, finely mashed
3 ounces cream cheese, softened
1 6-ounce can crushed pineapple, in own juice, drained
1 cup sugar
1 teaspoon vanilla extract
1 20-ounce jar cherry pie filling

Preheat oven to 350°.   20 servings.

Combine everything except cherries. Pour into greased 9" x 13" pan. Bake 30 minutes. Add cherries and bake an additional 30 minutes.

VIVIAN'S APRICOT KUGEL (M)

1 pound medium noodles, cooked and drained
1/2 pound margarine
1/2 pound cream cheese, softened
8 medium eggs, beaten
3 tablespoons lemon juice
1 cup sugar

Set aside:

1/2 cup sugar
1 teaspoon ground cinnamon
3/4 pound dried apricots
1 6-ounce jar maraschino cherries

Preheat oven to 350°.   20 servings.

Cook apricots in boiling water until barely soft. Combine cinnamon and 1/2 cup of sugar. Set aside.

Melt margarine and cream cheese together. Combine noodles, margarine, cream cheese, eggs, lemon juice, and 1 cup of sugar.

In a greased 9" x 13" pan, place a layer of 1/2 of the apricots and 1/2 of the cut maraschino cherries. Combine cinnamon and sugar and sprinkle fruit with 1/2 of the mixture. Spread with a layer of 1/2 of the cheese and noodle mixture.

Repeat until finished. Top with remaining cinnamon-sugar mixture and cherries. Bake 1 hour.

PIÑA COLADA KUGEL (M)

1 pound fine noodles, cooked and drained
6 large eggs, beaten
1 pint sour cream
1 14-ounce can crushed pineapple, in own juice, not drained
1 cup sugar
1/2 teaspoon vanilla extract
1 cup shredded sweetened coconut
   dash cinnamon

Preheat oven to 350°.   20 servings.

Combine all ingredients. Pour into greased 9" x 13" pan,
sprinkle with cinnamon, and bake for 1 hour.

*To sweeten a fresh pineapple, twist off the leafy top and place
pineapple in microwave 3 minutes on high.*

BUTTERSCOTCH AND APRICOT KUGEL (M)

1 pound wide noodles, cooked and drained
1-1/2 cups dried apricots
2 cups milk
1 small box instant butterscotch pudding
1/2 pound cream cheese, softened
3/4 cup sugar
4 large eggs, beaten
1 teaspoon vanilla extract
2 tablespoons orange juice
1/2 pint sour cream

Topping:

1/4 pound butter, melted
2 cups crushed corn flakes
1/4 cup sugar
1 teaspoon ground cinnamon

Preheat oven to 350°.   20 servings.

Cook apricots in boiling water until barely soft. Prepare pudding with the milk and set aside.

In a large bowl cream together cream cheese and sugar. Add eggs, vanilla, orange juice and sour cream, mix together. Add pudding, mixing thoroughly. Add noodles.

Pour 1/2 mixture into a greased 9" x 13" pan. Cover with apricots. Add the rest of the noodle mixture.

Combine ingredients for topping and sprinkle over noodle mixture. Bake 1 hour. Top with cool whip for a luscious dessert.

CUSTARDY APRICOT KUGEL (M)

1/2 pound fine noodles, cooked and drained
1/2 pound cream cheese, softened
1 12-ounce-can apricot nectar
1/2 cup sugar
3 large eggs, beaten
1/4 pound butter or margarine, melted
1 cup milk

Topping:

4 tablespoons butter or margarine, melted
2 cups crushed corn flakes
1/4 cup brown sugar
1 teaspoon ground cinnamon

Preheat oven to 350°.   20 servings.

Beat together cream cheese, nectar, sugar, eggs, butter or margarine, and milk until smooth.

Add noodles and mix thoroughly. Pour into 9" x 13" pan sprayed with non-stick baking spray.

Combine ingredients for topping and sprinkle over noodle mixture. Bake 1 hour.

DAIRY APRICOT JAM KUGEL (M)

1/2 pound wide noodles, cooked and drained
3 ounces cream cheese, softened
3 large eggs, beaten
1/2 cup sugar
3/4 cup apricot jam
3/4 cup milk
6 tablespoons butter or margarine, melted

Topping:

1/4 pound butter or margarine, melted
2 cups crushed corn flakes
1/4 cup sugar
1 teaspoon ground cinnamon

Preheat oven to 350°.   20 servings.

Beat together everything except noodles. Add noodles. Spread mixture in greased 9" x 13" pan.

Combine topping ingredients and sprinkle over noodle mixture. May be refrigerated and baked the next day. Bake 45 to 60 minutes until browned and firm.

DON'T COOK THE NOODLES KUGEL (M)

1/2 pound medium noodles, uncooked
8 ounces cream cheese, softened
8 ounces sour cream
8 ounces cottage cheese
1-1/2 cups milk
1/4 pound butter or margarine, melted
1/4 cup sugar
4 large eggs, beaten
pinch salt

Preheat oven to 325°.   20 servings.

Butter 9" x 13" pan. Cover with dry noodles. Beat together cream cheese, sour cream, cottage cheese, and milk.

Add melted butter, sugar eggs and salt and mix thoroughly. Pour over noodles. Bake 45 to 55 minutes.

ABOUT HOW MY SISTER NANCY MAKES KUGEL (M)

I have written this recipe exactly the way my sister Nancy gave it to me. She is a great cook and doesn't get too hung up on recipes. She is always ready to improvise.

In a big bowl, mix with a spoon, not beater, 16 ounces cottage cheese, 16 ounces sour cream, about 6 beaten eggs, 1/2 cup (more or less) sugar, about 1/2 teaspoon cinnamon, 1 teaspoon vanilla. Add plumped raisins, if you like them...golden ones better than brown. Boil 8 to 10 ounces thin-noodles (about 3/8" wide) until al dente...drain them. Mix the concoction together with the noodles. Put it in a greased up pan...bake about 30 to 40 minutes at 325° to 350°, depending on how well your oven works...add crushed pineapple, cherries, or blueberries, smeared on top, after about 20 minutes, if you wish...Cool it off, serve with sour cream.

FARMER CHEESE, NUTS, AND RAISIN KUGEL (M)

  1/2 pound fine noodles, cooked and drained
  1 pint sour cream
  1/2 pound cream cheese, softened
  1 pound farmer cheese or large curd cottage cheese, drained
  4 large eggs, beaten
  1 cup sugar
  1 teaspoon vanilla extract

Topping:

  1/2 cup raisins
  1 teaspoon ground cinnamon
  1/2 cup chopped walnuts

Preheat oven to 350°.   20 servings.

Combine all ingredients except noodles and topping. Beat until smooth. Add noodles and mix thoroughly.

Pour into greased 9" x 13" pan and bake 30 minutes.

Remove from oven and sprinkle with topping ingredients. Bake for an additional 30 minutes.

WONDERFUL KUGEL SOUFFLÉ (M)

  8 ounces medium noodles, cooked and drained
  1 cup sugar
  8 ounces cream cheese, softened
  2 teaspoons vanilla extract
  8 medium eggs, beaten
  1 pint sour cream
1-1/2 sticks butter or margarine, softened

Preheat oven to 350°.   20 servings.

Continued on next page.

Wonderful Kugel Soufflé continued.

Beat together all ingredients, except noodles, until smooth. Greased a 9" x 13" pan and line noodles on the bottom. Pour egg mixture on top of noodles. Do not stir to combine.

Topping:

Combine 1/2 cup sugar and 1 teaspoon ground cinnamon and sprinkle over top of kugel mixture before baking.

OR use:

1   20-ounce can prepared blueberry pie filling.

Bake 45 minutes until puffy and browned like a soufflé. If pie filling is used, spread on to after baking.

APPLE AND RAISIN NOODLE KUGEL (M)

      1   pound medium noodles, cooked and drained
      3   large eggs, beaten
      3   tablespoons butter or margarine, melted
1-1/4   cups cottage cheese
   1/2   cup sour cream
   1/2   cup milk
      1   cup sweet apples, pared and chopped
1-1/4   teaspoon grated lemon rind
   1/2   cup each sugar and raisins
   1/2   teaspoon ground cinnamon
   1/2   teaspoon ground nutmeg
   1/2   teaspoon salt

Preheat oven to 350°.   8 servings.

Combine all ingredients except nutmeg. Pour into greased 2-1/2 quart casserole.

Sprinkle top with nutmeg. Bake 40 to 50 minutes. Serve hot as is or top with jelly.

LIKE-A-CINNAMON BUN KUGEL (M)

This kugel is oozing with scrumptiousness.

1/2 pound medium noodles, cooked and drained
3 large eggs, separated
1/2 pint sour cream
1/2 pound cottage cheese
1/2 cup milk
1/2 cup sugar
1 6-ounce can crushed pineapple, in own juice, drained

For bottom of pan:

1/4 pound butter or margarine
1/2 cup brown sugar
1/2 cup chopped walnuts
1/3 cup white raisins
1-1/2 teaspoons ground cinnamon

Preheat oven to 350°.   10 servings.

Combine sour cream, cottage cheese, milk, sugar, and pineapple. Add beaten egg yolks and mix thoroughly.

Stir in noodles and fold in stiffly beaten egg whites.

Melt butter in a 10" x 10" pan and spread evenly, coating bottom and sides. Sprinkle with brown sugar, cinnamon, walnuts, and raisins, and stir thoroughly.

Pour noodle mixture on top. Bake 1 hour. Invert onto serving dish when done. Garnish with more white raisins.

MAGNIFICENT KUGEL (M)

1 pound medium noodles, cooked and drained
5 large eggs, separated
4 tablespoons butter or margarine, melted
1 cup cottage cheese
1 cup light sour cream
1 teaspoon vanilla extract
1/4 cup honey
3 tablespoons orange juice
1 tablespoon grated orange rind
3 tablespoons lemon juice
1 teaspoon grated lemon rind
3 tablespoons dark brown sugar
1 teaspoon ground cinnamon
1/4 teaspoon allspice
2 medium tart apples, pared and coarsely chopped
1 cup soft pitted prunes, chopped
1 cup pitted dates, chopped
1 cup pineapple tidbits, in own juice, drained
1/2 cup golden seedless raisins
1/2 cup walnuts, chopped
   pinch salt

Preheat oven to 350°.   24 servings.

Beat together egg yolks, butter, cottage cheese, sour cream, vanilla extract, honey, orange juice, orange rind, lemon juice, and lemon rind. Add brown sugar, salt, cinnamon, and allspice, and beat again.

Add egg mixture to noodles and mix thoroughly.

Combine fruit and nuts and add to noodle mixture. Stir thoroughly. Fold in stiffly beaten egg whites.

Pour into greased 11" x 15" baking pan. Cover with foil and bake 30 minutes. Uncover and bake 15 or 20 minutes or until set. Serve hot.

BLINTZ SOUFFLÉ (M)

12 cheese blintzes, uncooked, commercially packaged or
    home-made (p. 187)
1/4 pound butter or margarine, softened
  1 teaspoon ground cinnamon
  1 teaspoon vanilla extract
1/2 cup sugar
  5 large eggs, beaten
  1 pint sour cream

Preheat oven to 350°.   6 servings.

Arrange blintzes in 9"x 13" pan, one or two layers high.

Combine butter, cinnamon, vanilla, sugar, eggs, and sour
cream and mix thoroughly. Pour liquid mixture over blintzes.
Bake 45 minutes or until top is set.

Le soufflé
magnifique!
Une photo?

HOW DID THERE GET TO BE SO MANY RECIPES?

Once upon a time (this is true), in the "Old Country," people did not measure ingredients as they do today. They would show how the food was prepared to anyone who was interested and say, as my grandmother did, "you use a little bit of this and a little bit of that" (the Yiddish expression is sheet a rhine). Or people would say, "use a handful, a dash or a pinch and bake it in the oven" (no length of time was given). Rough estimates were used and people were remarkably successful in making very tasty dishes.

Although pounds and ounces eventually became used, there were no standard measuring cups and spoons, as we have today. If the use of a spoon or cup was mentioned when giving recipes, my Bubbie (grandmother), Gittle Rosenthal Finklestein, always referred to her favorite huge soupspoon or tiny, little teaspoon or her favorite glass that she used for cooking and baking. Some people measured by using eggshells. After cleaning and drying the shells, they used them as measuring devices.

Since nobody really knew for sure exactly how much of this or that was to be used, they estimated. The recipes were altered as they were passed to others, something like whispering down the line.

NOT SWEET
DAIRY NOODLE KUGEL

Also see: Broccoli/Spinach Kugel, p. 88
Dairy Onion Noodle Kugel, p. 93
Mushroom and Sour Cream Kugel, p. 90

CHEDDAR CHEESE KUGEL (M)

This kugel tastes like macaroni and cheese, but better!
It has southwestern cuisine possibilities.

1   pound medium egg noodles, cooked and drained
1/2 cup butter or margarine, melted
4   large eggs, beaten
2   cups sour cream
1   pound cheddar cheese, grated
1/3 cup bottled jalepeño peppers, chopped, drained (optional)
     salt and pepper, to taste

Preheat oven to 350°.   20 servings.

Combine all ingredients and mix thoroughly. Pour into lightly
greased 9" x 13" pan. Bake 1 hour.

"KUGEL MAKES IT BIG OFF BROADWAY"

The romantic comedy entitled "Beau Jest," produced by Arthur Cantor, made its debut off Broadway in New York City at the Lambs Theater in October, 1991. It has since appeared in theaters around the country. When it came to the Society Hill Playhouse in my home town (Philadelphia) for six months in September of 1992, I was invited by the producers to be a special guest at a performance.

Kugel has an important role in the show and is sometimes served at intermission. The playhouse sponsored a kugel contest and compiled a <u>Kugel Contest Cookbook.</u> The producers gave me permission to use the following recipe in my cookbook entitled <u>The Kugel Story — Not Just Noodle Pudding 2</u>, the mother of this book.

SAVORY SOCIETY HILL KUGEL (M)

1/2 pound wide egg noodles, cooked and drained
2 cups scallions, sliced
4 garlic cloves, peeled and crushed
1/4 cup butter or margarine, melted
4 eggs, beaten
1 pound creamed cottage cheese, at room temperature
1 cup light sour cream, at room temperature
1/2 teaspoon salt
1/4 teaspoon pepper
1-1/2 cups Muenster cheese, grated
1/4 cup wheat germ mixed with 1/4 teaspoon paprika

Preheat oven to 350°.   20 servings.

Sauté scallions and garlic in melted butter until limp. Toss noodles with scallion mixture.

Combine eggs, cottage cheese, sour cream, salt and pepper, and stir into noodle mixture. Pour into lightly greased 9" x 13" pan.

Sprinkle top with Muenster cheese and dust the cheese evenly with wheat germ mixture. Bake 40-45 minutes.

NOT TOO SWEET CUSTARD KUGEL (M)

1 pound noodles, cooked and drained
1/4 cup sugar
2 large eggs, beaten
1/4 pound butter or margarine, softened
1 teaspoon vanilla extract

Topping:

1/2 pound cottage cheese
1 cup sour cream
2 large eggs, beaten
1/4 cup milk
1 teaspoon lemon juice

Preheat oven to 350°.   20 servings.

Beat together sugar, eggs, butter, and vanilla. Add noodles and mix thoroughly. Pour into ungreased 9" x 13" pan. Beat together topping ingredients. Pour over noodle mixture. Bake 1 hour.

EASY NOT SWEET DAIRY KUGEL (M)

1/2 pound fine noodles, cooked and drained
3/4 cup sour cream
4 large eggs, beaten
2 tablespoons sugar
1 teaspoon salt
1 pint cottage cheese

Topping:

3 tablespoons butter or margarine, melted
4 tablespoons dry breadcrumbs

Preheat oven to 375°.   10 servings.

Beat together eggs, sour cream, salt, and sugar. Add cottage cheese and noodles. Pour into greased 10" x 10" baking dish. Sprinkle with breadcrumbs and butter. Bake 40 minutes.

LAYERED NOODLE PUDDING (M)

1 pound broad noodles, cooked and drained
1 pound small curd cottage cheese, drained
4 large egg yolks, beaten
1/2 cup heavy cream
2 tablespoons sugar
1 teaspoon salt

Topping:

1/4 cup breadcrumbs
4 tablespoons butter or margarine, melted

Preheat oven to 375°.   20 servings.

Beat together cottage cheese, egg yolks, cream, sugar, and salt until smooth.

In 9" x 13" pan sprayed with baking spray, arrange alternate layers of noodles and cheese mixture, starting and ending with noodles. Sprinkle with breadcrumbs and butter. Bake 30 minutes.

RICOTTA CHEESE KUGEL (M)

8 ounces wide noodles, cooked and drained
4 large eggs, beaten
1/4 pound butter or margarine, softened
3 ounces cream cheese, softened
1 pint sour cream
1 cup ricotta cheese
3 tablespoons sugar
1 cup white raisins, plumped in hot water, drained
3 tablespoons lemon juice

Continued on next page.

69

Ricotta Cheese Kugel continued.

<u>Topping</u>:

1 cup corn flakes
4 tablespoons butter or margarine, melted

Preheat oven to 350°.   10 servings.

In food processor that has been fitted with steel blade, mix together eggs, 1/4 pound butter, cream cheese, sour cream, ricotta cheese, sugar, and lemon juice until smooth.

Pour into large mixing bowl and fold in noodles and raisins. Pour into greased 10" x 10" baking dish. Sprinkle corn flakes on top and drizzle with melted butter. Bake 1 hour. Serve hot.

TANGY SOUR CREAM KUGEL (M)

8 ounces medium egg noodles, cooked and drained
1 tablespoon canola oil
2 tablespoons butter or margarine, melted
3 large eggs, separated
1 tablespoon sugar
1 pint sour cream
    dash dry mustard
    salt, to taste

Preheat oven to 350°.   8 servings.

Melt butter with oil and add to noodles. Stir in beaten egg yolks, sugar, sour cream, dry mustard, and salt.

Beat egg whites until stiff, and fold into noodle mixture. Pour in noodle mixture into 8" x 8" pan that has been lightly sprayed with baking spray. Bake 1 to 1-1/2 hours until brown.

BUTTERMILK KUGEL (M)

12 ounces wide noodles, cooked and drained
4 large eggs, beaten
4 cups buttermilk
1 pound small curd cottage cheese
1 teaspoon sugar
2 tablespoons butter or margarine, melted
  salt and pepper, to taste

Preheat oven to 400°.   20 servings.

Spread drained noodles evenly on the bottom of a greased 9" x 13" pan. Beat together remaining ingredients and pour over noodles. Dot with additional butter. Bake 1 hour. Serve with sour cream and sweetened, sliced fresh strawberries.

GREEN NOODLE KUGEL (M)

8 ounces broken spinach noodles, cooked and drained
1 cup farmer cheese or large curd cottage cheese, drained
1 clove garlic, chopped
1 cup sour cream
1 onion, finely minced
1 tablespoon Worcestershire sauce
  salt, to taste
  dash of Tabasco sauce

Topping:

1 cup sour cream to serve on the side
  grated Parmesan cheese for sprinkling

Preheat oven to 350°.   8 servings.

Break noodles into 2-1/2-inch pieces and cook until tender. Drain noodles and combine with cottage or farmer cheese, garlic, sour cream, onion, Worcestershire sauce, Tabasco, and salt. Pour mixture into greased 10" x 10" pan. Bake about 45 minutes, until brown and crusty on top. Serve with Parmesan cheese and additional sour cream.

PAREVE NOODLE KUGEL

Pareve noodle kugels are Ashkenazic in origin. Some of the oldest recipes have been traced to the early Middle Ages in Germany. To be kosher, pareve margarine or oil may be used in pareve (P) recipes, but never butter. If butter is used, the food must be considered milchig (M) or dairy.

SWEET PAREVE NOODLE KUGEL

For many years at the Jewish Community Center of Central Florida in Maitland (north of Orlando), during their Hanukkah festival, there was a Chicken Soup and Kugel Kontest. I had the honor of being a judge in 1992. The Award Winning Chicken Soup recipe is on p. 161.

AWARD WINNING KUGEL (P)

8 ounces wide noodles, cooked and drained
2 medium sweet apples, pared and diced
1/2 cup white raisins
1/2 cup dried apricots, diced
1/2 cup prunes, diced
6 tablespoons sugar
9 tablespoons canola oil
4 large eggs, beaten

Preheat oven to 350°.   20 servings.

Mix all ingredients and pour into a well-oiled 9" x 13" pan. Sprinkle with cinnamon and sugar. Bake 40 minutes.

ORANGE AND APPLE KUGEL (P)

1 pound fine noodles, parboiled and drained
8 medium eggs, beaten
4 large sweet apples, pared and sliced
1 cup raisins
1 cup orange juice
2 tablespoons grated orange rind
1 carrot, grated
1 teaspoon baking powder
1/4 teaspoon salt
1 cup brown sugar
1 teaspoon vanilla extract
1/2 cup applesauce

Preheat oven to 350°.   24 servings.

Combine all ingredients together and mix thoroughly. Pour into greased 11" x 15" baking pan. Bake 1 hour.

APPLE, RAISIN, AND NUT KUGEL (P)

1 pound wide noodles, cooked and drained
6 large eggs, beaten
6 tablespoons pareve margarine, melted
1/2 teaspoon ground cinnamon
5 medium sweet apples, pared and diced
1/3 cup brown sugar
3/4 cup chopped walnuts
2 tablespoons lemon juice
1/2 cup raisins or currants
1/2 cup maraschino cherries
  scant capful almond extract

Preheat oven to 350°.   20 servings.

Combine all ingredients except cherries. Mix thoroughly. Pour into 9" x 13" baking pan sprayed with baking spray. Garnish with cherries. Bake 50 minutes or until set and golden brown.

APPLE AND PINEAPPLE KUGEL (P)

10 ounces wide noodles, cooked and drained
3 large eggs, beaten
3/4 cup sugar
1 14-ounce can crushed pineapple, in own juice, drained
5 medium sweet apples, pared and diced
1/4 cup canola oil

Topping:

1 6-ounce jar maraschino cherries
dash cinnamon

Preheat oven to 350°.   20 servings.

Combine noodles, eggs, sugar, pineapple, and apples; mix thoroughly.

Heat oil in 9" x 13" pan. Pour mixed ingredients into pan. Decorate with maraschino cherries. Sprinkle cinnamon on top. Bake 1 hour. Best if baked the day before serving and refrigerated overnight. Freezes well.

APPLESAUCE AND JAM KUGEL (P)

1/4 pound noodles, cooked 5 to 8 minutes and drained
1/2 stick pareve margarine
6 large eggs, beaten
4 tablespoons brown sugar
1 pint applesauce

Topping:

1 cup corn flakes, crushed
1/2 cup jam (peach, apricot or prickly pear*)

Preheat oven to 350°.   20 servings.

Continued on next page.

74

Applesauce and Jam Kugel continued.

Add margarine to noodles and stir. Add beaten eggs, sugar, and applesauce. Pour into greased 9" x 13" pan. Bake for 45 minutes.

Remove pan from oven and spread top of kugel with jam. Top with corn flakes and return to oven for 30 minutes.

*Prickly pear jam, also known as cactus jam, is available in the southwest and in specialty food stores throughout the United States. Native Israelis are called "Sabras" after this delicious fruit, which is prickly and hard on the outside, sweet and soft on the inside.

STRAWBERRY, PINEAPPLE, APPLE KUGEL (P)

1/2 pound medium noodles, cooked and drained
1 apple, peeled and grated
5 large eggs, separated
1/2 cup strawberry preserves
1 8-ounce can crushed pineapple, in own juice, drained
2 tablespoons honey

Topping:

1/4 cup pareve margarine
1/2 cup strawberry preserves
dash cinnamon and sugar

Preheat oven to 350°.   10 servings.

Combine apple, egg yolks, 1/2-cup preserves, pineapple, and honey. Add noodles and mix thoroughly.

Beat egg whites until stiff but not dry; fold into noodle mixture. Pour into greased 10" x 10" pan.

Dot top with margarine, cinnamon, sugar, and dabs of the rest of the preserves. Bake 45 minutes, cool 5 minutes, and serve.

CHERRY AND RAISIN KUGEL (P)

1 pound medium noodles, cooked and drained
3/4 cup dark raisins
10 maraschino cherries, diced
3/4 cup canola oil
1 tablespoon grated lemon rind
3 tablespoon lemon juice
8 medium eggs, beaten
1 teaspoon vanilla extract
1 cup sugar
   dash cinnamon

Preheat oven to 350°.   20 servings.

Combine everything except cinnamon. Stir well and pour into greased 9" x 13" pan. Sprinkle with cinnamon. Bake 45 minutes. Serve hot or cold.

PINEAPPLE, APPLESAUCE, AND RAISIN KUGEL (P)

1 pound wide noodles, cooked and drained
3/4 cup sugar
1 6-ounce can crushed pineapple, in own juice, not drained
1 15-ounce can applesauce
2 cups apple juice
1/4 pound pareve margarine
1 cup non-dairy liquid creamer
1/2 cup raisins
1 tablespoon vanilla extract
5 large eggs, beaten

Preheat oven to 350°.   20 servings.

Combine everything. Pour mixture into greased 9" x 13" pan. Sprinkle with cinnamon and sugar, if desired. Bake 45 minutes.

LEMON AND PINEAPPLE KUGEL (P)

8 ounces wide noodles, cooked 12 minutes and drained
1 cup raisins
8 ounces crushed pineapple, in own juice, drained
3 tablespoons lemon juice
4 large eggs, beaten
1/2 cup each brown and white sugar
1 teaspoon salt

Preheat oven to 350°.   8 servings.

Combine all ingredients and mix thoroughly. Pour into greased 8" x 8" baking pan.

Topping:

1 teaspoon ground cinnamon
1 tablespoon sugar
1 cup bread crumbs
2 tablespoons pareve margarine, melted
2 teaspoons grated lemon rind
1 tablespoon lemon juice

Combine topping ingredients, mix thoroughly, and spread noodle mixture. Bake 45 minutes until top is browned.

NADINE'S FRUITY KUGEL (P)

1 pound wide noodles, cooked and drained
6 large eggs, beaten
1 cup sugar
1 teaspoon vanilla extract
1/4 pound pareve margarine
1 6-ounce can crushed pineapple, in own juice, drained*
1 30-ounce can fruit cocktail, in own juice, drained*

Preheat oven to 350°.   20 servings.

Continued on next page.

Nadine's Fruity Kugel continued.

Combine noodles with all ingredients and mix thoroughly. Grease 9" x 13" pan with baking spray and pour in mixture. Bake 1 hour.

*Variation:

Use 1 14-ounce can crushed pineapple and 1 11-ounce can drained mandarin oranges instead of fruits mentioned in recir^

JERUSALEM KUGEL (P)

This spicy kugel, which combines Ashkenazic and Sephardic cooking styles, is very popular in Jerusalem The women of Mea Shearim make this kugel in huge quantities and sell it. It is also now available throughout Israel in grocery stores.

12 ounces fine noodles, parboiled and drained
 3 medium eggs, beaten
 2 teaspoons freshly ground black pepper
1/2 cup canola oil, divided
1/4 cup sugar
 1 teaspoon salt

Preheat oven to 175°.   8 servings.

Toss noodles with 1/4-cup of the oil; cover to keep warm. Place sugar and remaining 1/4 cup of oil in a saucepan; heat over a low flame. Caramelize by cooking for about 20 minutes, occasionally shaking pan. Do not stir.

When sugar caramelizes, slowly pour it over the warm noodles. Mix thoroughly. Add eggs, salt, and pepper and stir. Pour into greased 8" x 8" pan. Cover and bake overnight or up to 14 hours. Serve warm.

SWEET AND HOT KUGEL (P)

Sweet and peppery, this kugel is a variation of the Jerusalem Kugel. In February of 1991 I brought it to the world premiere of the show entitled "Sweet and Hot in Harlem," a spectacular review of Harold Arlen's music. My cousin, Robert Cohen, was the producer. The cast liked the kugel so much that I had to bake it for them again when they appeared later that year in Buffalo, New York.

      1 pound thin spaghetti, broken, cooked and drained
    1/2 pound pareve margarine
      1 cup brown sugar
      6 large eggs, beaten
  2-1/2 teaspoons freshly ground black pepper
      1 teaspoon salt

Preheat oven to 350°.   10 servings.

Cook margarine and sugar in a large pan, gently stirring for 5 minutes until sugar begins to caramelize.

Add spaghetti immediately. Add eggs, salt, and pepper. Pour into lightly greased 10" x 10" pan. Bake 1 hour.

ASSORTED FRUIT KUGEL (P)

      1 pound broad noodles, cooked and drained
    1/3 cup orange juice
      3 large eggs, beaten
      1 tablespoon grated orange rind
      1 cup sugar
      3 tablespoons lemon juice
      2 medium tart apples, pared and grated
      2 tablespoons grated lemon rind
    1/2 pound pitted and cut prunes
    1/2 cup raisins
      1 cup small dried apricots
    1/2 cup pareve margarine, melted

Continued on next page.

79

Topping:

1/4 cup pareve margarine, melted
1/4 cup matzo meal
1/4 cup brown sugar

Preheat oven to 350°.   20 servings.

Combine all ingredients, except topping, with cooked noodles and stir thoroughly. Pour into a 9" x 13" baking pan sprayed with baking spray. Mix topping ingredients and sprinkle over noodle mixture. Bake 1 hour.

DRIED FRUIT AND NUT MIX KUGEL (P)

8 ounces medium noodles, cooked and drained
1/4 cup canola oil
4 large eggs, beaten
1/4 cup sugar
1/4 cup pineapple or apricot jam
1 cup orange juice
1/2 teaspoon ground cinnamon
1/4 teaspoon ground ginger
6 ounces dried fruit and nut mix
1 sweet apple with skin, diced
  pinch salt

Preheat oven to 350°.   10 servings.

Pour 1/2 of the oil over noodles and toss. Beat together eggs, sugar, and remaining oil.

Add jam, orange juice, cinnamon, ginger, and salt. Stir in dried fruit and apple. Add noodles and stir mixture thoroughly.

Pour mixture into greased 10" x 10" pan. Cover with foil and bake for 40 minutes. Remove foil and bake 20 minutes more until firm and set. Serve warm or at room temperature.

APRICOT NOODLE PUDDING (P)

1 cup dried apricots
1/2 pound broad noodles, cooked and drained
3 large eggs, beaten
1/2 cup sugar
1 teaspoon salt
1/4 cup pareve margarine
1/4 cup graham cracker crumbs
1 teaspoon cinnamon

Preheat oven to 350°.   9 servings.

Soak apricots in boiling water until soft. Beat eggs, sugar, and salt until creamy; add to noodles. Drain soaked apricots and sprinkle with graham cracker crumbs mixed with cinnamon, saving a little for topping.

Melt margarine in glass 9" x 9" baking pan and add 1/2 of the noodle mixture. Spread apricots over noodle mixture; add remaining noodles. Sprinkle graham cracker crumbs and cinnamon mixture on top. Bake 40 minutes until browned.

PAREVE APRICOT JAM KUGEL (P)

1/2 pound wide noodles, cooked and drained
3 teaspoons mayonnaise
3 large eggs, beaten
1/2 cup sugar
3/4 cup apricot jam
3/4 cup pareve liquid creamer
6 tablespoons pareve margarine, melted

Preheat oven to 350°.   20 servings.

Combine mayonnaise, eggs, sugar, jam, creamer, and margarine. Beat well and add to noodles. Spread in greased 9" x 13" pan. Add topping.

Continued on next page.

Pareve Apricot Jam Kugel continued.

Topping:

1/4 pound margarine, melted
2 cups crushed corn flakes
1/4 cup sugar
1 teaspoon ground cinnamon

Combine ingredients for topping and sprinkle over noodle mixture. May be refrigerated at this point and baked the next day. Bake 45 to 60 minutes until browned and firm.

GORGEOUS BUNDT PAN PECAN KUGEL (P)

1/2 pound broad noodles
1/4 cup pareve margarine, melted
1/2 cup brown sugar
1/2 cup pecan halves
1/2 cup pecans, chopped
1/2 cup white sugar
2 large eggs, beaten
1/4 cup pareve margarine, melted
1/2 teaspoon ground cinnamon
1/2 teaspoon salt

Preheat oven to 350°.   8 servings.

Mix margarine with brown sugar. Place on bottom of a bundt pan.

Arrange pecan halves with pretty side down. Mix noodles with remaining ingredients.

Pour into pan and bake 40 minutes. Invert onto serving platter. Great for dessert. Serve with fruit salad.

CONFECTIONERS' SUGAR KUGEL (P)

1/2 pound fine noodles, cooked and drained
4 large eggs, separated
1 cup confectioners' sugar
2 tablespoons grated almonds
   allspice for sprinkling

Preheat oven to 350°.   8 servings.

Beat egg yolks and sugar. Add almonds and noodles. Fold in stiffly beaten egg whites. Pour into greased 8" x 8" pan. Sprinkle with allspice. Set into pan filled 1 inch deep with water and bake 1/2 hour.

NOT SWEET PAREVE NOODLE KUGEL

Also See: Ashkenazic Salt and Pepper Kugel, p. 27
            Diet Vegetable Noodle Kugel, p. 85
            Vegetable Kugel Section, p. 88
            Onion Kugel Section, p. 92

THE KUGEL SONG
By Nina Yellin,
Arranged by Melody Blasenheim

The first time I saw ku-gel I cried out oh wow yum! It looked like cake I'd ne-ver baked and I be-gan to hum! mmm! I tas-ted my first mor-sel It went down smooth as silk I could not stop I ate some more then drank a glass of milk! mmm!

DIETETIC KUGEL

See: Food Substitutes, p. 243

DIET DON'T COOK THE NOODLES KUGEL (M)

12 ounces thin noodles, <u>uncooked</u>
 1 teaspoon vanilla extract
 3 large eggs, beaten
1/2 cup sugar
 2 cups skim milk
16 ounces low-fat cottage cheese

Preheat oven to 350°.   70 calories   20 servings.

Combine all ingredients and mix thoroughly. Grease 9" x 13" pan with baking spray and pour in mixture. Bake for 45 minutes.

DIET VEGETABLE NOODLE KUGEL (P)

1 pound medium noodles, cooked and drained
2 cups yellow onions, chopped
2 cups mixed green and red peppers, chopped
3 cups carrots, grated
2 tablespoons canola oil
5 large eggs, beaten
1 teaspoon freshly ground black pepper
  salt or to taste

Preheat oven to 350°.   70 calories   20 servings.

In large pan, sauté onions and peppers in oil. Toss in carrots (if too dry, add about 2 tablespoons of water). Do not overcook vegetables — they should just be a little bit soft.

Add salt and pepper, then eggs and noodles.

Pour into 9" x 13" baking pan sprayed with baking spray. Bake 45 minutes to 1 hour or until browned on top.

DIET APPLE KUGEL (M)

    2 cups cooked thin or medium noodles
  2/3 cup low-fat cottage cheese
    2 large eggs, beaten
    1 tablespoon light margarine, melted
  1/2 teaspoon ground cinnamon
  2/3 cup nonfat dry milk
1-1/2 cups water
    2 teaspoons lemon juice
1-1/2 teaspoons vanilla extract
    2 small sweet apples, pared and coarsely chopped
      heat-stable sweetener equivalent to 6 teaspoons sugar

Preheat oven to 350°.   140 calories   8 servings.

Combine all ingredients except noodles and apples and mix
with blender or food processor until smooth. Pour into a large
mixing bowl, and stir in noodles and apples.

Grease 8" x 8" pan with baking spray and pour in mixture.
Sprinkle with additional cinnamon. Bake 1 hour, uncovered,
until set and lightly browned.

DIET PASSOVER CARROT KUGEL (F)

1-1/2 cups matzo, crumbled
    1 cup kosher for Passover chicken bouillon
    3 large eggs, beaten
1-1/2 cups grated carrots, tightly packed
    1 tablespoon Passover oil
    1 tablespoon dry onion flakes
  1/2 teaspoon salt
    2 teaspoons parsley, minced

Preheat oven to 325°.   75 calories   6 servings.

Combine matzo, chicken bouillon, and eggs. Sauté carrots in
oil and sprinkle with salt, parsley, and onion flakes.

Pour into 1-1/2 quart baking dish. Bake 50 minutes or until
firm.

DIET PINEAPPLE CHEESECAKE KUGEL (M)

1 cup thin noodles, cooked and drained
2 large eggs, beaten
2/3 cup low-fat cottage cheese
1/2 cup plain low-fat yogurt
2 teaspoons vanilla extract
1 teaspoon vanilla butternut flavoring
1/4 teaspoon ground cinnamon
1 cup crushed pineapple, in own juice, drained
    heat-stable sweetener equivalent to 6 teaspoons sugar

Preheat oven to 325°.   90 calories   8 servings.

In blender, combine eggs, cottage cheese, sweetener, yogurt, vanilla, vanilla butternut flavor, and cinnamon. Blend until smooth.

Pour into mixing bowl; add pineapple, and noodles, and stir thoroughly.

Pour mixture into 8" x 8" baking pan sprayed with baking spray. Sprinkle with additional cinnamon. Bake 40 minutes until set.

VEGETABLE KUGEL

Also see: Chicken Soup Matzo Kugel, p. 126
Carrot Pudding, p. 123
Diet Passover Carrot Kugel, p. 86
Diet Vegetable Noodle Kugel, p. 85
Passover Carrot Kugel, p. 123
Onion Kugel Section, p. 91

BROCCOLI/SPINACH KUGEL (M OR P)

12 ounces medium noodles, cooked and drained
1 pint sour cream (or 1-1/2 cups pareve non-dairy creamer)
2 packages pareve kosher onion soup mix
4 whole large eggs, beaten
4 egg whites, beaten
1 cup unsweetened applesauce
2 packages chopped frozen spinach OR broccoli, cooked and
drained, and squeezed dry (don't mix vegetables, use 2
packages of either)
dash freshly ground black pepper

Optional Topping:

1 cup corn flakes, whole or crushed

Preheat oven to 375°.   15 servings.

Combine sour cream, soup mix, eggs, egg whites, pepper, and applesauce.

Add noodles and vegetable and mix thoroughly.

Top with corn flakes, if desired. Pour into greased 9" x 13" pan. Bake about 1 hour until firm and browned.

BEAUTIFUL ZUCCHINI KUGEL (P)

3 zucchini, pared
2 bunches broccoli, stalks only
2 carrots
1 white all-purpose potato
1 large yellow onion
3 large eggs, beaten
1/3 cup canola oil
1-1/2 teaspoons salt
    dash freshly ground black pepper

Preheat oven to 350°.   9 servings.

Grate zucchini, broccoli stalks, carrots, potato, and onion. Beat together eggs, oil, salt, and pepper and combine with vegetables.

Pour into 9-inch baking pan sprayed with non-stick baking spray. Bake 1-1/2 hours until solid and golden. Do not freeze.

UGLY ZUCCHINI KUGEL (P)

Tastes great, just looks bad!

2 medium zucchini, pared, grated, and drained
2 teaspoons sugar
1/4 teaspoon salt
1 teaspoon ground cinnamon
1/2 cup raisins
1/4 cup chopped walnuts
3 tablespoons canola oil or pareve margarine
1 small onion, finely chopped
4 large eggs, beaten lightly

Preheat oven to 350°.   8 servings.

Combine sugar, salt, cinnamon, raisins, walnuts, and zucchini.

Sauté onion in oil until golden and add to zucchini mixture with eggs. Pour into greased 8" x 8" baking dish. Bake 40 minutes until lightly browned. Do not freeze.

SPINACH KUGEL WITH ORZO (M)

    1 cup orzo pasta, cooked and drained
    4 large eggs, beaten
    1/2 teaspoon Worcestershire sauce
    1/4 teaspoon freshly ground black pepper
    1 cup ricotta cheese
    1 cup fresh grated Parmesan cheese
    1 package chopped frozen spinach, cooked
    1/3 cup dry bread crumbs

Preheat oven to 350°.   8 servings.

Pour cooked spinach into a colander and press with paper towels to remove excess moisture. Beat together 3 of the eggs, Worcestershire sauce, and pepper; add cheeses, spinach, and orzo.

Grease a 9" x 9" pan and sprinkle evenly with breadcrumbs. Pour mixture into pan. Beat remaining egg and brush on top of mixture. Bake for 45 minutes.

MUSHROOM AND SOUR CREAM KUGEL (M)

    8 ounces medium noodles, parboiled and drained
    1 large yellow onion, chopped
    1/2 pound fresh button mushrooms, chopped
    4 tablespoons canola oil
    3/4 teaspoon paprika
    2 large eggs, beaten
    1 cup sour cream
    3 tablespoons fresh parsley, chopped
      salt and freshly ground black pepper, to taste

Preheat oven to 350°.   10 servings.

Sauté onions and mushrooms in oil until onions are browned. Add salt, pepper, and 1/4 teaspoon of the paprika. Combine eggs, sour cream, parsley, onion mixture, and noodles. Pour into greased 10" x 10" pan. Sprinkle with remaining 1/2 teaspoon of paprika. Bake 30 minutes. Serve topped with sour cream.

MOCK POTATO KUGEL (M OR P)

Made with "flower" things.

1 large head of cauli"flower," finely chopped
1 medium yellow onion, chopped
5 large eggs, beaten
1/4 teaspoon ground white pepper
3 tablespoons saf"flower" oil
1/4 teaspoon nutmeg
1/3 cup wheat "flower" or 4 tablespoons potato starch

Topping:

2 *tablespoons apricot preserves*
1 cup applesauce (optional)
OR
4 ounces American style cheese (optional)
sun"flower" seeds, enough to sprinkle over top

Preheat oven to 350°.   9 servings.

Finely chop cauliflower and onion in a food processor using the steel blade.

Add eggs, pepper, and nutmeg. Add wheat flour and oil; mix.

Pour into 9" x 9" pan sprayed with non-stick baking spray. Top with seeds. Bake 1 hour until golden brown.

Serve topped with applesauce, or for a dairy kugel, melt Velveeta Cheese over top. Do not freeze.

ONION KUGEL

ONIONS AND KUGEL

You may have noticed in the "Vegetable Kugel" section that most vegetable kugel recipes include onions. However, there are enough onion kugel recipes in this book to qualify for a section of their own.

Onions have been popular in Jewish cooking for thousands of years. They grew almost everywhere in the Diaspora, were easy to preserve, and were used in many ways — as seasoning and eaten alone as a vegetable. Yemenites ate them for dessert, candied.

There are many varieties. I usually use the yellow or white kind in recipes. Although raw white onions have a slightly bitter taste, they sweeten when cooked. Vidalia onions, which have a short spring season, purple, and Spanish onions are great for sandwiches and salads.

Onions have been scientifically proven good for the heart, especially if eaten in conjunction with garlic. However, they do have a negative effect on some people's digestive systems and their breath. Therefore, I suggest that you eat onions in moderation.

Tzibble (onion) kugels have probably been around for as long as there have been kugels. Actually, I had never heard of tzibble kugel until I started collecting recipes for this book. When I mentioned it to Mom Yellin, she was ecstatic. She loves it but had never prepared one and had not eaten tzibble kugel in many, many years. So, being the good daughter that I am, I made one for her! She was a very happy mom.

TZIBBLE KUGEL (P)

5 large eggs, separated
2 cups yellow onions, finely chopped
1/2 cup canola oil (Passover oil during that holiday)
1/2 cup matzo meal
    pinch salt and pepper

Preheat oven to 350°.   8 servings.

Beat egg yolks. Add onion, oil, matzo meal, salt, and pepper. Mix well.

Beat egg whites to form stiff peaks and fold into mixture.

Pour into greased 8" x 8" pan. Bake 30 minutes.

DAIRY ONION NOODLE KUGEL (M)

1 pound wide noodles, cooked and drained
1/4 pound butter, melted
8 ounces cream cheese, softened
1 pint sour cream
1 large white onion, chopped
4 large eggs, beaten
1/4 cup breadcrumbs
    salt and pepper, to taste

Preheat oven to 350°.   10 servings.

Combine all ingredients and stir thoroughly.

Pour into greased 10" x 10" baking pan. Sprinkle with breadcrumbs and paprika, and dot with butter. Bake 1 hour.

BARLEY AND ONION KUGEL (F)

4 cups kosher consommé, chicken or beef
1 cup pearl barley
2 teaspoons salt
1/2 pound chopped button mushrooms
2 large onions, diced
2 tablespoons canola oil
1/4 teaspoon freshly ground black pepper
2 large eggs, beaten

Preheat oven to 350°.   8 servings.

Boil consommé and stir in salt and barley. Cover and cook 45 minutes or until soft, stirring occasionally. Drain excess water.

Brown onions and mushrooms in oil and add to barley. Add pepper and eggs.

Pour into greased 8" x 8" pan. Bake 40 minutes or until browned and set.

RAISIN AND ONION KUGEL (P)

1 pound medium noodles, cooked and drained
1/2 cup white raisins, chopped
1 medium white onion, chopped
4 tablespoons pareve margarine
4 large eggs, beaten

Preheat oven to 375°.

Soak raisins in cold water for 15 minutes.

Brown onions in margarine, and allow to cool. Add eggs, noodles, and raisins.

Pour into greased 8" x 8" pan and bake for 40 minutes.

MUSHROOM AND ONION KUGEL (F)

8 ounces wide noodles, parboiled and drained
4 large onions, diced
1 cup button mushrooms, diced
5 tablespoons canola oil
2 tablespoons flour, unbleached and presifted
1 cup kosher chicken bouillon
2 large eggs, beaten
   salt and pepper, to taste
   paprika

Preheat oven to 350°.   10 servings.

Brown mushrooms and onions in oil; add flour. Prepare bouillon and slowly stir in until mixture is thick. Add to noodles. Season to taste with salt and pepper.

Pour into greased 10" x 10" pan. Pour eggs over top and sprinkle with paprika. Bake 30 minutes. Top with additional browned mushrooms and onions, if desired.

SWEET ONION KUGEL (P)

1 pound medium noodles, cooked and drained
2 large white onions, chopped
1/4 cup canola oil, divided
2 teaspoons dark brown sugar
3 large eggs, beaten
1/2 cup breadcrumbs
1/4 teaspoon salt
1/4 teaspoon freshly ground black pepper

Topping:

1/3 cup brown sugar
2 tablespoons pareve margarine

Continued on next page.

Sweet Onion Kugel continued.

Preheat oven to 350°.   20 servings.

Grease 9" x 13" baking pan with 2 tablespoons of the oil and place in oven while oven is preheating, about 10 minutes.

Sauté onions in remaining 2 tablespoons oil. Combine with noodles, eggs, brown sugar, breadcrumbs, salt, and pepper.

Pour mixture into warmed pan. Sprinkle with brown sugar and dot with margarine and apricot preserves. Bake for 40 minutes until browned and crispy.

KASHA AND ONION KUGEL (P)

    1 pound medium noodles, cooked and drained
    1 cup kasha (groats), cooked
    4 large eggs, beaten
    4 large white onions, chopped
1/4 pound fresh button mushrooms, sliced
    1 clove garlic, chopped
1/3 cup pareve margarine
1/3 cup canola oil
1/2 teaspoon salt
1/2 teaspoon freshly ground black pepper

Preheat oven to 350°.   20 servings.

Combine kasha, noodles, and eggs.

In heavy skillet, melt margarine and add oil. Sauté onions, mushrooms, and garlic; add salt and pepper.

Add onion mixture to kasha mixture and mix well. Pour into greased 9" x 13" pan and bake for 45 minutes.

STOVETOP COOKING

Many noodle, bread, and potato kugel recipes can be prepared stovetop.

Pour mixture into a well-oiled deep skillet, press mixture down and cover pan. Cook over slow fire; do not stir. When mixture starts to set, shake pan. When firm and crusty, put a plate or fry pan lid on top. Hold lid with one hand and flip pan upside down to allow mixture to come out of pan; carefully slide kugel upside down back into pan. Brown so the entire kugel is crusty. If necessary, place a plate on top of flipped kugel to hold it down while browning the final portion.

STOVETOP CHICKEN LIVER AND ONION KUGEL (F)

1 pound medium noodles, cooked and drained
8 large eggs, beaten
1 medium yellow onion, chopped
1/2 pound chicken-livers*
1/2 cup canola oil
1 teaspoon fresh dill
  dash of salt, pepper, and garlic powder

10 servings.

Sauté onions in oil. Rinse chicken livers under cold water and broil until browned. Dice chicken livers and combine with onions.

Sprinkle with salt, pepper, garlic powder, and dill. Add eggs and noodles. Cook stovetop.

Some cuts of meat must be broiled to abide by laws of kashruth. Liver is one of those meats.

POTATO KUGEL

Also see: Mock Potato Kugel, p. 91

Because potatoes are inexpensive, easy to grow, and very filling, they became a staple food of the Ashkenazic Jews. Potato latkes (pancakes) made with grated potatoes, eggs, and onions, and fried in goose fat became a popular item and a traditional Hanukkah food. The same batter was poured into pottery crocks or baking tins and was baked in a slow oven overnight for the Sabbath. This became known as "potato kugel."

Pop Yellin came from a large and poor family (nine kids). His dad died when he was 12 years old. Because potatoes were so inexpensive, his mother prepared them in every possible way and they were served very often as the main course. On the Sabbath, she prepared them Pop's favorite way, in a kugel.

Pop Field also came from a large, poor family (eight kids). When his mom made potato kugel, she made it crisp and browned on the outside with a thick crust. It was soft and wonderful on the inside. She made her kugel in a heavy iron skillet on top of the stove.

The beverage for the evening was a glass of "2 cents plain." When my father was a very young boy, he would be sent to the corner soda shop with a beautiful pitcher that is now sitting in my china cabinet. The kindly soda man would fill it with seltzer for 2 cents. When Dad was a little older, the squirt bottles came into existence, which I remember from my childhood. About 13 years ago, my Aunt Myrna told me they could still be found in stores in Florida and New York. I have more recently seen them in antique stores.

FAVORITE POTATO KUGEL (P)

This batter can also be used to make potato pancakes.

12 medium white potatoes with skin, grated and well drained
2 large yellow onions
2 large carrots, brushed and grated
1/4 cup matzo meal
1 tablespoon salt
1/2 teaspoon ground white pepper
4 large eggs, beaten*
1/4 cup canola oil

Preheat oven to 375°.   20 servings.

Grate potatoes and vegetables in food processor. Drain mixture thoroughly and pour into large mixing bowl.

Add remaining ingredients and mix thoroughly.

Pour into oiled 9" x 13" baking pan. Bake 1 hour or until top is browned and crisp at edges. Do not freeze.

*For lighter kugel, separate eggs. Add beaten egg yolks and 2 teaspoons baking powder. Fold stiffly beaten egg whites into potato mixture.

SWEET POTATO KUGEL (P)

  1 cup carrots, brushed and grated
1-1/2 cups fresh sweet potatoes, pared and grated
  1 cup white all purpose potatoes, pared and grated
  1 tart apple, pared and grated
  1 cup raisins
1/2 cup brown sugar
  1 cup flour
3/4 cup margarine, melted
  1 teaspoon baking soda
1/4 teaspoon cinnamon
1/2 teaspoon salt
  1 teaspoon nutmeg

Preheat oven to 325°.   10 servings.

Combine all ingredients and mix well. Spray a 10" x 10" baking dish with non-stick baking spray. Pour mixture into baking dish. Cover with aluminum foil and bake for 45 minutes. Raise oven temperature to 350°, remove foil, and bake and additional 15 minutes. Serve warm. Do not freeze.

EASY CHEESY POTATO KUGEL (M)

  3 large eggs, beaten
  2 cups water
  1 6-ounce package potato pancake mix
  1 pound small curd cottage cheese
3/4 cup sour cream

Preheat oven to 350°.   8 servings.

Combine eggs, water, and potato pancake mix; allow to thicken for about 3 minutes. Stir in cottage cheese and sour cream. Pour into greased 8" x 8" baking pan and bake for 1 hour until edges brown.

MASHED POTATO KUGEL (P)

4 cups white potatoes, cooked and drained, and mashed
4 large eggs, beaten
2 tablespoons uncooked grits or farina
4 tablespoons pareve margarine
1 teaspoon onion powder
   salt and pepper, to taste

Preheat oven to 375°.   8 servings.

Combine all ingredients and mix well. Pour mixture into a greased 8" x 8" baking pan and bake 45 minutes or until browned.

CREAM CHEESE AND POTATO KUGEL (M)

4 medium white potatoes, grated
8 ounces cream cheese, softened
3 large eggs, beaten
1/4 cup margarine, melted
1/4 cup flour, unbleached and presifted
1/2 teaspoon baking powder
1/2 teaspoon salt
1/4 cup white onion, chopped

Preheat oven to 350°.   8 servings.

Blend together cream cheese, eggs, and margarine.

Add flour, baking powder, and salt. Stir in potatoes and onions and mix thoroughly. Pour into greased 8" x 8" baking pan and bake for 50 minutes.

BREAD AND GRAIN KUGEL

Also see: Kugel, p. 29
Kasha and Onion Kugel, p. 96

PYOTA GREEK STYLE FARINA KUGEL (M)

3-1/2 cups boiling water
  2/3 cup instant Cream of Wheat cereal (farina) or grits
    1 cup nonfat dry milk powder
    2 tablespoons butter, small pieces
  1/2 cup sugar
  1/3 cup honey
  1/2 teaspoon vanilla extract
  1/4 teaspoon ground cinnamon
    5 large eggs, beaten
      fresh fruit for topping (optional)

Preheat oven to 325°.   10 servings.

Stir cereal and milk powder into boiling water. Lower heat to medium and cook cereal stirring continuously until thick (about 5 minutes).

Remove from heat and add butter, sugar, honey, vanilla, and cinnamon.

While beating eggs, add 1 cup of cereal mixture. Stir egg mixture into rest of cereal mixture.

Pour into greased 10" x 10" pan and sprinkle top with cinnamon. Bake 1 hour or until inserted knife comes out clean. Serve cold topped with fresh fruit, if desired.

MIDDLE EASTERN FARINA KUGEL (P)

Tastes like Matzo Meal Pancakes. Puffy like a soufflé.

1/2 cup instant Cream of Wheat cereal (farina) or grits
 2 cups boiling water
 1 tablespoon pareve margarine
1/2 cup sugar
1/2 teaspoon salt
 1 teaspoon grated lemon rind
 5 large eggs, separated

Preheat oven to 350°.   10 servings.

Stir farina into boiling water. Lower heat to medium and cook cereal stirring continuously until thick, about 5 minutes. Remove from heat and add margarine, sugar, and salt and let cool.

Mix lemon rind and egg yolks into farina mixture. Beat egg whites until stiff and fold in. Grease a 10" x 10" pan and pour in mixture. Bake 30 minutes.

MILLET KUGEL (P)

Millet can be purchased at most health food stores and can sometimes be found in bulk food sections in supermarkets.

 3 cups water
 1 cup millet grains
 2 cups celery, diced
 2 cups grated apple, with skin
 2 large eggs, beaten
 1 cup raisins
1/2 cup sunflower seeds
1/2 teaspoon ground cinnamon
 2 teaspoons grated orange rind
1/2 teaspoon light salt
1/2 teaspoon vanilla extract

Continued on next page.

Millet Kugel continued.

Preheat oven to 350°.   10 servings.

In a large heavy skillet, bring water to a boil. Add millet gradually while stirring. Reduce heat to simmer and cook for 30 minutes or until all the water is absorbed.

Stir remaining ingredients into cooked millet. Pour mixture into 10" x 10" baking pan sprayed with nonstick baking spray. Sprinkle lightly with cinnamon. Bake about 30 minutes.

For a dairy breakfast, serve topped with your favorite yogurt.

BULGUR AND NUT KUGEL (P)

        2 cups bulgur
        5 cups water
     3/4 cup sugar
        2 large eggs, well beaten
     1/4 cup honey
        2 cups ground walnuts or almonds
        1 tablespoon ground cinnamon
     1/2 teaspoon light salt

Preheat oven to 350°.   10 servings.

Boil water and add bulgur. Reduce heat to simmer and cook for 30 minutes, stirring frequently.

Add remaining ingredients and mix well. Pour into greased 10" x 10" baking pan. Bake 40 minutes.

CORNMEAL KUGEL (M)

Although my definition of kugel states that corn is never used as an ingredient, cornmeal works. When this is hot, its texture is very much like cornbread.. As it cools, it becomes more like kugel, somewhere between cheesecake and bread.

     1 cup cornmeal
     1 cup flour, unbleached and presifted
     1 teaspoon baking powder
    1/2 teaspoon salt
    1/2 cup small curd cottage cheese
  1-1/2 cups plain yogurt
  1-1/2 cups sour cream
    1/4 cup butter or margarine, softened
    3/4 cup sugar
     3 large eggs, separated

Preheat oven to 350°.   8 servings.

In a small bowl, combine first four ingredients. In a medium bowl, combine cottage cheese, sour cream, and yogurt. In a large bowl, cream butter with 1/2 cup sugar. Add egg yolks and beat until smooth. Stir in cheese mixture alternating with dry ingredients.

In a small glass bowl, whip egg whites until they form soft peaks. Add remaining 1/4 cup sugar and beat until egg whites are stiff and shiny but not dry. Fold egg whites gently into cheese mixture. Pour into greased 8" x 8" baking pan. Bake 45 minutes or until center comes out dry. Serve warm with sour cream.

CREAMY RICE KUGEL (M)

1   cup white rice, cooked
5   large eggs, beaten
2-1/2   cups whole milk
1   12-ounce can evaporated milk
8   ounces cream cheese, softened
1/4   pound butter or margarine, softened
1/4   cup sugar
1   cup white raisins
1   tablespoon vanilla flavoring
2-1/2   teaspoons ground cinnamon

Preheat oven to 350°.   9 servings.

Combine rice, eggs, milks, cream cheese, butter or margarine, and sugar. Add raisins, vanilla, and cinnamon and mix well. Pour into greased 9" x 9" pan. Bake for 1-1/4 hours until top is golden. Serve cold.

PINEAPPLE, RAISIN AND NUT RICE KUGEL (P)

3   cups rice, white or brown (not instant), cooked
1/2   cup white sugar
1/2   cup brown sugar
1/4   cup canola oil
1   teaspoon grated lemon rind
1   teaspoon ground cinnamon
1/2   teaspoon vanilla extract
3   large eggs, beaten
1/2   cup raisins
1/2   cup crushed pineapple, in own juice, not drained
1/2   cup walnuts, chopped

Preheat oven to 350°.   8 servings.

Beat together sugars, oil, lemon rind, cinnamon, and vanilla. Add eggs, one at a time, then rice, combining thoroughly. Stir in raisins, pineapple, and walnuts.

Pour into greased 8" x 8" pan. Bake 1 hour or until golden. Serve warm or cold with whipped cream for dairy dessert.

ORANGE RICE KUGEL (M)

3 cups rice, white or brown (not instant), cooked
1 cup light cream
1 cup orange juice
1/4 cup orange liqueur
4 large eggs, beaten
1/2 cup sugar
1 teaspoon grated orange rind
1/4 teaspoon allspice
1 11-ounce can mandarin oranges, drained
2 tablespoons flour, unbleached and presifted
3/4 cup raisins
1/2 teaspoon salt

Preheat oven to 375°.   10 servings.

Combine everything and mix thoroughly. Pour into greased
10" x 10" pan and bake 1 hour. Serve warm topped with
whipped cream for dessert.

FRUIT AND NUT BREAD KUGEL (P)

8 slices hallah, cubed
1/2 cup pareve margarine
1 cup sugar
4 large eggs, beaten
1 20-ounce can crushed pineapple, in own juice, drained
1/3 cup walnuts, chopped
1 tart apple, pared and thinly sliced
2 tablespoons wheat germ
  dash cinnamon

Preheat oven to 350°.   10 servings.

Cream together margarine, sugar, and eggs. Add bread,
pineapple, nuts, and apple.

Pour into greased 10" x 10" pan. Sprinkle with wheat germ
and cinnamon. Bake for 1 hour or until brown.

MOM YELLIN'S BREAD STUFFING KUGEL (P or F)

Poultry stuffing, filling or dressing (however you say it), when baked outside the bird in a baking pan, casserole dish or prepared stovetop (p. 97) can also be called kugel. You will save about 600 calories.

1	large green bell pepper, diced
1	large yellow onion, diced
2	stalks celery, without leaves, diced*
1/4	pound pareve margarine or 1/2 cup chicken broth
1	small loaf hallah with crust, torn into pieces
5	large eggs or 10 egg whites
	dash garlic powder, salt, pepper, and paprika

Preheat oven to 350°.   8 servings.

Sauté green pepper, onion, and celery in margarine or chicken broth. Sprinkle generously with garlic powder, salt, pepper, and paprika.

Break bread into large chunks and place in large mixing bowl. Add vegetable mixture and stir. Add margarine or broth and eggs or egg whites to thoroughly moisten bread. Knead mixture with your hands.

Pour into well-greased casserole pan. Bake about 1 hour until firm and browned or cook stovetop (p.96).

*Variation:

Use 2 cups shredded carrots and 1 cup of sliced mushrooms instead of celery, or add broiled chopped chicken-liver and other gizzards.

CHOLENT KUGEL

Also see: Cholent, p. 181
Steamed 3-Bowl Apple Kugel, p. 120

Since the Middle Ages in Central and Eastern Europe, people have been baking steamed kugel in a round covered earthenware or metal pot in the center or on top of cholent.

Cholent (stew) has been around for at least 2,500 years and was served at the earliest Sabbaths. Every town and family seemed to have their own favorite ways of preparing cholent, which is probably as versatile as kugel.

The ingredients, in many different combinations, would be beans, peas, rice, potatoes, and/or barley. Vegetables such as carrots, turnips, green beans, and onions are added along with a variety of herbs and spices. Meat or poultry can also be included. The amount of meat one added, in early times in Poland and Russia, was a sign of how wealthy the family was.

Sweet kugel became the official noontime Sabbath dessert. If baked overnight together with cholent, the entire meal would be ready to eat after Saturday morning religious services or at "schul ende," as it would be referred to in Yiddish. The word "cholent" is possibly derived from this expression. Or it may have been taken from the French word "chaud" or the Hebrew word "chamim," both meaning "hot."

Since cooking is not permitted on the Sabbath in a very religious home, the cholent-and-kugel was prepared and partially cooked before sundown on Friday. It was then baked overnight on a low flame to prevent it from burning. To help retain the juices, the meal was covered with cheesecloth or sealed with a dough made of flour and water. Plenty of water was added to allow for evaporation. Water cannot be added on the Sabbath since that would be considered work.

The pots were taken to the baker who marked them with the owner's name. Young non-Jewish boys would deliver the meals after synagogue. Frequently there were mistakes and the true owner would not get the meal she or he had prepared. Not to worry — the other meal was probably wonderful and recipes were exchanged later!

Although work is not permitted on the Sabbath, carrying is allowed within the home. In small villages (shtetls), a wire called the "Eruv" was used to enclose the community. This made the village "one household" where carrying was permitted. If the wire broke, the food was passed from house to house until it reached its owner.

RUMANIAN KUGEL BALLS (P)

      1 cup cornmeal
    1/2 cup boiling water
      1 cup flour, unbleached and presifted
      2 tablespoons sugar
  1-1/2 teaspoons salt
    1/2 teaspoon paprika
    1/4 teaspoon freshly ground black pepper
    1/2 cup canola oil

6 servings.

Stir together cornmeal and water. Slowly add flour; add remaining ingredients and thoroughly mix. Drop heaping tablespoons of this mixture into cholent and cover with the hot liquid.

FRUIT AND SPICE KUGEL (P)

8 cups stale bread crumbs
4 tablespoons water
6 tablespoons sweet red wine
2 large eggs, beaten
2 medium sweet apples, with skin, diced
2 pears, with skin, diced
6 plums, peeled and diced
1/4 cup raisins
1/2 cup canola oil
3 tablespoons lemon juice
1 tablespoon grated lemon rind
1 teaspoon ground cinnamon
1 teaspoon allspice
1/2 teaspoon ground cloves
1/2 teaspoon salt

Preheat oven to 250°.   10 servings.

Sprinkle water and 1/2 of the wine over breadcrumbs; mix well. Combine remaining ingredients and stir into crumb mixture.

Pour into greased 10" x 10" baking pan. Cover and bake overnight in the center of a cholent, or in pan filled halfway with water.

111

THIS NEEDS SOME GRAVY KUGEL (P)

1/2 cup bread crumbs
2 cups flour, unbleached and presifted
8 ounces kosher shortening
2 large eggs, beaten
1/2 teaspoon salt
1/2 teaspoon freshly ground black pepper

Preheat oven to 450°.   8 servings.

Sprinkle a greased 2-quart casserole dish with breadcrumbs. Combine shortening, flour, eggs, salt and pepper.

Pour mixture into dish. Cover with heavy foil and bake 30 minutes. Reduce heat to 375° and bake 2 more hours, or at 250° for 4 hours in a pan in the center of a cholent mixture.

STEAMED PEAR KUGEL (P)

Filling:

3 firm pears, pared and sliced
1/2 cup raisins
4 prunes, diced
1 teaspoon ground cinnamon
1/2 cup sugar
pinch ground nutmeg
pinch salt

Dough:

1-1/2 cups flour, presifted
1/4 teaspoon salt
2 teaspoon baking powder
1 teaspoon sugar
2 large eggs, beaten
4 tablespoons pareve margarine, divided

Continued next page.

112

Steamed Pear Kugel continued.

Preheat oven to 250°.   6 servings.

Soak pitted prunes in warm water until plump. Combine with pears, raisins, and spices. Set aside.

Sift flour, salt, baking powder, and sugar together. Add 2 tablespoons of margarine and eggs and work into a medium to loose dough with your hands or food processor. Add water, 1 tablespoon at a time, if too stiff. If too loose, add flour, 1 tablespoon at a time. Dough should be soft.

Knead dough into a ball. Roll with floured rolling-pin to about 1/8" thickness. Spread filling mixture over dough. Dot with remaining margarine.

Fold edges in toward center, pinching into the shape of a ball. With a wide spatula, transfer to a greased 2-quart baking dish.

Set dish into center of cholent pan. Surround with cholent ingredients. Or place baking dish in a pan of hot water. Cover kugel tightly with foil and bake 4-5 hours or overnight.

As water or cholent liquid evaporates, add more water so that kugel will brown slowly and not burn.

PASSOVER KUGEL

KUGEL FOR PASSOVER?

Jewish law states that all processed foods must be specially prepared and approved for Passover. In order to uphold the laws of kashruth (being kosher) for this holiday, Passover kugel recipes use only potatoes, matzo, a derivative of matzo, or special Passover noodles as a base.

Processed food must be approved "kosher for Passover."

✡ Only use kosher for Passover oil, margarine, and jams.
✡ In pareve Passover recipes, use pareve and kosher for Passover margarine.
✡ Extracts are not kosher for Passover.
✡ Potato starch and baking soda are pure products and not leavening agents and can be used for Passover.

SWEET PASSOVER KUGEL
Also see: Ugly Zucchini Kugel, p. 89

CINNAMON AND RAISIN MATZO KUGEL (M)

4 cups matzo farfel, soaked and drained
5 eggs, separated
1/4 cup sugar
1 cup skim milk
1 pound cottage cheese
3 tablespoons Passover margarine, melted
1 teaspoon salt
2 teaspoons ground cinnamon
1/2 cup raisins (optional)
1 cup sour cream

Preheat oven to 350°.   15 servings.

Continued on next page.

Cinnamon and Raisin Matzo Kugel continued.

Mix together everything except egg whites.

Beat egg whites until stiff and fold into matzo mixture. Pour into greased 9" x 13" pan. Bake 40 minutes. Serve warm with sour cream for topping.

MATZO KUGEL WITH APPLES AND NUTS (P)

6 matzot (egg or plain), soaked and drained
6 large eggs, separated
1 cup sugar or honey
1/2 teaspoon ground cinnamon
1/3 cup orange juice
1/3 cup lemon juice
1 tablespoon grated lemon rind
1/2 cup raisins (optional)
6 medium tart apples, pared and thinly sliced
1 cup chopped walnuts or slivered almonds
1/2 cup pareve Passover margarine, melted
    cinnamon and sugar for sprinkling

Preheat oven to 350°.   15 servings.

Beat together egg yolks, sugar or honey, and cinnamon.

Stir in juices, rind, matzo, raisins, apples, walnuts, and margarine.

Beat egg whites until stiff and fold into mixture. Sprinkle with cinnamon and sugar. Bake in greased 9" x 13" pan 45 minutes.

PINEAPPLE UPSIDE-DOWN MATZO KUGEL (M)

5 egg matzot, broken into small pieces
6 large eggs, beaten
1/4 cup milk
1/2 cup butter, divided
3/4 cup brown sugar, divided
8 pineapple rings in own juice, drained
1/2 teaspoon salt
1/2 teaspoon ground cinnamon
1/4 teaspoon ground ginger
3 tablespoons lemon juice
2 teaspoons grated lemon rind
1/2 cup chopped walnuts
1/2 cup chopped dried fruit (prunes, apricots, or dates)
1/2 cup raisins

Preheat oven to 350°.   9 servings.

Beat 3 eggs and combine with milk. Soak matzo pieces in mixture; set aside.

Melt 1/4 cup of the butter in oven in bottom of 9" x 9" pan. Remove from oven and sprinkle with 1/4 cup brown sugar. Place pineapple rings on top.

Beat the other 3 eggs and add remaining melted butter, remaining 1/2 cup brown sugar, salt, cinnamon, ginger, lemon juice, and lemon rind. Beat thoroughly.

Add nuts and matzo mixture and fold in dried fruit and raisins.

Pour mixture into greased 9" x 13" pan. Sprinkle with additional cinnamon and sugar. Bake for 45 minutes until golden brown. Let sit 5 minutes. Loosen edges and invert over serving dish.

MATZO MEAL KUGEL (P)

3/4 cup matzo meal
6 large eggs, separated
1/4 cup cold water
1/4 cup Passover oil
1/4 teaspoon ground pepper
1/2 teaspoon salt
1/4 cup sugar

Preheat oven to 350°.   8 servings.

Beat egg yolks with water. Add everything except egg whites.
Beat egg whites until stiff, not dry, and fold into mixture. Pour
into greased 8" x 8" pan and bake 1/2 hour.

DAIRY MATZO KUGEL (M)

5 matzot
2 cups sour cream
2 cups large-curd cottage cheese, well drained
3 large eggs, beaten
1/4 cup sugar
1 tablespoon grated orange rind
1/3 cup orange juice

Preheat oven to 350°.   8 servings.

Rinse matzo (do not soak); set aside. Mix together remaining
ingredients.

In a greased 8" x 8" pan, layer matzo and sour cream mixture,
ending with sour cream mixture. Bake 40 minutes.

117

DIET DAIRY MATZO KUGEL (M)

3 matzot
1 pound farmer cheese or low-fat cottage cheese
4 large egg whites, beaten
6 packs heat-stable artificial sweetener
1 teaspoon ground cinnamon
1 cup skim milk
1 tablespoon Passover margarine

Preheat oven to 350°.   160 calories   4 servings.

Mix cottage cheese, egg whites, sweetener, and cinnamon together. Pour milk into 8" x 8" pan and soak matzot (each one separately) about 2 minutes. Set matzot aside; save leftover milk. Clean baking pan and spray with non-stick baking spray.

Place 1 piece of matzo on bottom of pan and pour half of cottage cheese mixture over it. Repeat the layering with another matzo and the rest of the cottage cheese mixture. Top with third matzo. Dot with pieces of margarine. Cover everything with the saved milk. Bake uncovered 35-40 minutes or until set and golden.

MATZO KUGEL WITH PRUNES AND APRICOTS (P)

6 matzot
12 ounces prunes, pitted
6 ounces dried apricots
3 cups water
2 teaspoons salt
2 medium apples, pared and grated
6 large eggs, beaten
1/4 cup sugar

Preheat oven to 350°.   15 servings.

Cook prunes and apricots 5 minutes in water and drain; save 2 cups of the water. Soak matzot in the reserved water. Add all the remaining ingredients. Spoon into greased 9" x 13" pan. Bake until browned, about 1 hour.

BANANA YOGURT KUGEL (M)

6 matzot, broken, soaked and squeezed
4 large eggs, beaten
2/3 cup sugar
1 cup banana yogurt
1 cup dairy sour cream
1/2 cup crushed pineapple in own juice, drained
1 teaspoon vanilla extract
1 teaspoon ground cinnamon
1 cup mashed ripe bananas or fresh sliced strawberries

Topping:

1 tablespoon sugar
1 teaspoon ground cinnamon
2 tablespoons Passover margarine
1 11-ounce jar apricot or pineapple preserves, melted

Preheat oven to 350°.   10 servings.

Combine matzot, eggs, sugar, yogurt, sour cream, pineapple, vanilla, cinnamon, and bananas or strawberries.

Pour into a greased 10" x 10" baking pan. Combine sugar and cinnamon and sprinkle over kugel; dot with margarine.

Bake 45 minutes until center is firm. Heat preserves to melt and then brush over kugel. Serve warm.

STEAMED 3-BOWL APPLE KUGEL (P)

First Bowl – Combine in a small bowl:
2/3 cup brown sugar
4 teaspoons Passover oil

Second Bowl — Combine in a large bowl:
5 matzot, broken, soaked and drained
2 medium tart apples, pared and grated
2 teaspoons ground cinnamon
3 teaspoons sugar
1 teaspoon grated lemon rind
2 large eggs, beaten

Third Bowl — Combine in a medium bowl:
4 medium sweet apples, peeled and sliced
2 tablespoons lemon juice
1 cup raisins
4 tablespoons Passover apricot or peach jam
1/4 cup sugar

Preheat oven to 325°.   9 servings.

Grease a 9" x 9" pan and spread with first mixture. Top with half of second mixture, followed by all of third mixture. End with balance of second mixture.

Set in the center of a roasting pan and surround with water or a cholent (p. 181).

Bake 1-1/4 hours. Serve hot as a side dish or as dessert.

PEACH, APPLE, AND RAISIN FARFEL KUGEL (P)

Tastes like a cobbler.

1/2 cup matzo farfel, soaked and drained
1/2 cup matzo meal
1/4 cup sugar
 1 16-ounce can sliced peaches, drained
1/2 stick pareve Passover margarine, melted
 2 large eggs, beaten
 3 medium tart apples, pared and diced
1/2 cup raisins
    cinnamon and sugar for topping

Preheat oven to 350°.   8 servings.

Mix together all ingredients except cinnamon and sugar.

Pour into 8" x 8" pan sprayed with non-stick baking spray. Sprinkle with cinnamon and sugar.

Bake 45 minutes. Serve as a side dish with poultry or topped with ice cream as a dairy dessert,.

MATZO FARFEL AND WINE KUGEL (P)

 3 cups matzo farfel, soaked and drained
 3 large eggs, separated
2/3 cup sugar
1/4 cup sweet red wine
 1 teaspoon salt
 3 tablespoons Passover oil
 2 teaspoons grated orange rind

Preheat oven to 350°.   8 servings.

Soak farfel or matzo in cold water, then drain. Beat yolks with sugar and add wine, salt, orange rind, and oil. Mix into farfel.

Fold stiffly beaten egg whites into mixture. Pour into greased 8" x 8" pan and bake 30 minutes.

MATZO KUGEL WITH WHITE WINE SAUCE (P)

6 matzot, broken, soaked, and squeezed
6 large eggs, separated
1/2 cup sugar
2 teaspoons vanilla extract
1 teaspoon grated lemon rind
1 tablespoon lemon juice
4 medium tart apples, pared and cubed
1/2 cup dark raisins
1/2 cup white raisins
1 cup sliced almonds
4 tablespoons pareve Passover margarine

Preheat oven to 350°. 12 servings.

Break matzot into small pieces and soak in water until soft; drain and squeeze.

Beat egg yolks about 5 minutes. Add sugar, vanilla, lemon rind, and lemon juice and mix thoroughly. Add soaked matzo, apples, raisins, and almonds.

Beat egg whites until stiff and fold into mixture. Pour into greased a 10" x 10" pan and dot with margarine. Bake 50 minutes until browned. Serve with white wine sauce.

WHITE WINE SAUCE (P)

3/4 cup sugar
6 medium egg yolks, beaten
1 cup kosher for Passover dry white wine
2 teaspoons potato starch

In saucepan on top of a double boiler, slowly add sugar to beaten yolks.

Gradually add wine and potato starch. Stir continuously until mixture begins to thicken (about 10 minutes). Serve hot or cold. Can be refrigerated for 24 hours.

CARROT PUDDING (P)

1 cup matzo meal
1 teaspoon salt
1 teaspoon baking soda
1/2 cup brown sugar
1/2 cup Passover oil
3 large eggs, separated
3 cups raw carrots grated

Preheat oven to 350°.   8 servings.

Sift together matzo meal, salt, and baking soda. Cream sugar and oil. Beat egg yolks until light. Add egg yolks and dry ingredients alternately to creamed mixture and mix well.

Stir in carrots and fold in stiffly beaten egg whites. Bake in well-greased 8" x 8" pan 40 minutes.

PASSOVER CARROT KUGEL (P)

1/4 cup matzo meal
8 large eggs, separated
1 cup sugar
2 cups raw carrots, grated and tightly packed
1/2 cup tart apple, pared and shredded
1/2 cup sweet red wine
4 tablespoons lemon juice
4 teaspoons grated lemon rind
1/2 cup potato starch
1/2 cup chopped walnuts (optional)

Preheat oven to 375°.   15 servings.

Beat egg yolks with sugar until light. Add carrots, apple, wine, lemon juice, lemon rind, matzo meal, potato starch, and walnuts and mix thoroughly.

Beat egg whites until stiff and fold into carrot mixture. Spoon into 9" x 13" pan sprayed with non-stick baking spray and bake 35 to 40 minutes. Serve hot or cold.

PASSOVER FRUIT MEDLEY KUGEL (M)

4 cups matzo farfel
1-1/2 cups warm water
1/4 pound Passover margarine, melted
8 large eggs, beaten
1/4 teaspoon ground nutmeg
1/4 teaspoon ground cinnamon
1/2 cup plus 1 tablespoon sugar
8 ounces plain yogurt
8 ounces cottage cheese with pineapple
2 16-ounce cans peaches, drained, diced; reserve 1/2 cup
1 cup pitted dates, diced; reserve 1/4 cup

Topping:

1/2 cup peaches; reserved above
1/4 cup pitted dates; reserved above
2 tablespoons Passover margarine, melted
1/2 cup walnuts, chopped
1/4 cup matzo farfel
1 teaspoon cinnamon
1 tablespoon sugar

Preheat oven to 350°.   15 servings.

In large bowl, combine farfel and warm water; set aside.

Combine margarine, eggs, nutmeg, and sugar. Add yogurt, cottage cheese, and larger portion of peaches and dates.

Fold in soaked farfel until blended. Pour mixture into greased 9" x 13" baking pan.

Top with reserved peaches and dates. Combine 2 tablespoons of margarine, chopped walnuts, matzo farfel, cinnamon, and sugar. Sprinkle mixture evenly over kugel. Bake 40 to 45 minutes until set.

PASSOVER NOODLE FRUIT KUGEL (P)

1 1-pound box Passover noodles, cooked and drained*
2 tart apples, pared and sliced
1 20-ounce can crushed pineapple in own juice, drained
1/4 pound pareve Passover margarine, melted
4 large eggs, beaten
3/4 cup sugar
1 cup dried apricots, diced

Preheat oven to 375°.   9 servings.

Combine all ingredients. Pour into greased 9" x 9" pan. Bake 50 minutes.

*Note: Noodles made from derivatives of matzo can be found in some grocery stores during Passover. They may be used in any noodle kugel recipe that appears in this book.

NOT SWEET PASSOVER KUGEL

Also see: Tzibble Kugel, p. 93
Beautiful Zucchini Kugel, p. 89
Ugly Zucchini Kugel, p. 89
Potato Kugels, p. 98

PASSOVER SPINACH KUGEL (P)

1 cup white onions, chopped
1/2 cup celery, chopped
1/2 cup fresh mushrooms, sliced
1-1/2 cups carrots, grated
1 tablespoon pareve Passover margarine
2 packages frozen spinach, cooked and drained
3/4 cup matzo meal
3 large eggs, beaten
salt and pepper to taste

Preheat oven to 350°.   12 servings.

Sauté onion, celery, mushrooms, and carrots in margarine until tender. Add spinach, eggs, matzo meal, salt, and pepper. Pour into greased 10" x 10" pan. Bake for 45 minutes.

125

DIET PASSOVER CARROT KUGEL (F)

1-1/2 cups matzo, crumbled
1 cup kosher for Passover chicken bouillon
3 large eggs, beaten
1-1/2 cups grated carrots, tightly packed
1 tablespoon Passover oil
1 tablespoon dried onion flakes
1/2 teaspoon salt
2 teaspoons parsley, minced

Preheat oven to 325°.   75 calories.   6 servings.

Combine matzo and chicken bouillon; add eggs.

Sauté carrots in oil and sprinkle with salt, parsley, and onion flakes. Pour into 1-1/2 quart pan. Bake 50 minutes or until firm.

CHICKEN SOUP MATZO KUGEL (F)

6 matzot, rinsed and broken
2 large eggs, beaten
2-1/2 cups kosher for Passover chicken soup
1 large onion, diced
1/2 cup celery, diced
1/2 cup green pepper, diced
1/2 cup carrots, grated
4 tablespoons schmaltz (p. 127) or Passover oil
1/4 teaspoon salt
1/4 teaspoon ground pepper
1 teaspoon paprika
2 tablespoons parsley

Preheat oven to 350°.   8 servings.

Sauté onion, celery, green pepper, and carrots in schmaltz or oil and season with salt, pepper, paprika, and parsley.

Combine matzot, eggs, and chicken soup; add vegetables. Pour mixture into a greased 9" x 9" baking pan. Bake 1 hour.

MATZO KUGEL WITH LIVER (F)

4 matzot, soaked and squeezed
4 large eggs, beaten
2 large white onions, diced
2 tablespoons schmaltz (below) or Passover oil
1 pound chicken or beef liver, broiled
   dash salt and pepper

Preheat oven to 325°.   6 servings.

Combine matzot and eggs. Brown onions in oil or schmaltz.
Chop liver and combine with onions. Season with salt and
pepper.

Grease an 8" x 8" baking pan. Layer bottom of pan with half
of matzo mixture, add liver and onions, and top with
remaining matzo mixture. Bake 30 minutes or until browned.

SCHMALTZ AND GREBENES (F)

Schmaltz is rendered fat and the cooked skin is grebenes.
Although it is very tasty when used in recipes or spread on
matzo, very few people use schmaltz today.

Remove fat and fatty skin from chicken. For each cup of fat to
be rendered, you will need 1/4 cup of sliced onions and 1
apple slice. Wash and drain fat and skin and cut into small
pieces. Cook over low heat until fat is almost melted. Add
onions and apple and cook until onions are browned. Cool and
drain. Remove and discard apple slice. Onions and pieces of
skin (grebenes or cracklings) can be stored in refrigerator for
use in fleishig (F) kugel or other recipes.

KNISHES

KNISH WISH

When you wish upon a knish,
Makes no difference what the dish,
Potato, kasha, liver, rice,
Your meal will be nice.

Where happy hungry people meet,
And with vendors on the street,
That's where you'll find them.

Knishes at my mother's house,
At Mrs. Goldberg's with her spouse,
You've got to love them.

Sometimes they're served with the mustard,
Or sour cream,
Sometimes you've got to have them,
If only in your dreams.

KNISHES

Immigrants who arrived from Russia sometime around 1900 brought knishes to America. Knish (pronounced kin-ish) is a Yiddish word that was derived from the Russian knysh means "kind of bun." It is described in the <u>Oxford Dictionary of Foreign Words and Phrases</u> as "a baked or fried dumpling made of flaky dough with filling." The first knish bakery was founded in New York in 1910.

Knishes are almost as versatile as kugel. They are served warm as hors d'oeuvres, appetizers, snacks, a main course, or as a side dish with a meat or dairy meal. This tasty treat appears in just about every Jewish delicatessen in America. You can also find them in New York City where they are sold by street vendors with a side of spicy mustard. Cocktail-size knishes are about 2 inches around. When used as an appetizer, main course, or side dish, they are usually about 5 inches around and look something like half of a large baseball.

Although knishes do not come in as many varieties as kugel, there are many ways to make the filling and dough. Fillings are usually prepared with potato, meat, cheese, kasha, sauerkraut, rice, or a variety of vegetables.

KNISH DOUGH

CRISPY DOUGH (P)

4-1/2 cups flour, unbleached and presifted
2 large eggs, slightly beaten
1 cup canola oil
1 cup hot water

Makes 48 cocktail-size.

Mix all ingredients and knead for 5 minutes, until smooth. Cover with a cloth and set aside, or wrap in plastic wrap and refrigerate 30 minutes or overnight.

Divide dough into four balls. Place on floured board and roll to 1/8 inch thickness with floured rolling pin. Fill, shape, brush with oil, and place on ungreased baking sheet. Use with kasha, potato, liver, and vegetable fillings.

CELIA ELNER'S DOUGH (P)

4 cups flour, unbleached and presifted
4 large eggs, beaten
1/2 cup canola oil
1/4 teaspoon salt
1 teaspoon baking powder
1 tablespoon sugar
1/3 cup lukewarm water

Makes 24 large-size.

Beat eggs and oil together. Combine flour, salt, baking powder, and sugar. Make a well in center of flour mixture. Pour eggs mixture in the well and blend with a pastry cutter. Add water and knead with hands. Should form a soft, easy to handle ball. If too moist, add 1 tablespoon of flour at a time.

Divide dough into four balls. Place on floured board and roll to 1/8 inch thickness with floured rolling pin. Fill, shape, brush with oil, and place on ungreased baking sheet. Use with rice filling.

132

SOUR CREAM DOUGH (M)

3 cups flour, unbleached and presifted
2 teaspoons baking powder
1 teaspoon salt
1/2 pound butter or margarine
2/3 cup sour cream
2 teaspoon water, if needed

Makes 24 cocktail-size.

Combine flour, baking powder, salt, and butter in food processor and process until mixture looks like coarse meal. Add sour cream and process until dough holds together and forms sticky crumbs. Add water if dough is too dry.

Knead on a floured board until smooth. Cover and refrigerate for about 2 hours. Divide dough into four balls. Place on floured board and roll to 1/8 inch thickness with floured rolling pin. Fill, shape, brush with oil, and place on ungreased baking sheet. Use with cheese fillings.

STRUDEL DOUGH (P)

2-1/2 cups flour, unbleached and presifted
1 teaspoon baking powder
1/2 teaspoon salt
2 tablespoon sugar
1/4 cup canola oil
2 large eggs, beaten
1/2 cup warm water

Makes 24 cocktail-size.

Sift dry ingredients together. Add oil and eggs, and water to bind. Turn out onto a floured board. Knead until smooth and spongy. Set in bowl, sprinkle with flour, cover with plastic wrap, and chill 30 minutes or overnight.

Divide dough into four balls. Place on floured board and roll to 1/8 inch thickness with floured rolling pin. Fill, shape, brush with oil, and place on ungreased baking sheet.

FLAKY DOUGH (P)

1 cup pareve margarine
2 cups flour, unbleached and presifted
1/2 teaspoon salt
1/3 cup ice water
2 tablespoons vinegar
1 egg yolk

Makes 12 large-size.

Cut margarine into flour and salt with a pastry cutter. In separate bowl, combine water, vinegar, one egg yolk. Knead thoroughly until combined but do not overwork. Dough should be soft but not sticky. Cover dough with plastic wrap and chill for 2 hours.

Divide dough into four balls. Place on floured board and roll to 1/8 inch thickness with floured rolling pin. Fill, shape, brush with oil, and place on ungreased baking sheet.

FAT FREE DOUGH (P)

1 package dry active yeast
1/4 cup warm water
4 cups flour, unbleached and presifted
1/2 cup apple sauce
2 medium egg whites, unbeaten
1/2 cup sugar

Makes 30 cocktail-size.

Combine yeast and warm water with 1 teaspoon of the sugar in small bowl and allow to sit 10 minutes until foamy. In another small bowl, combine applesauce and 1/4 cup of the flour. In a large bowl, combine remaining flour with sugar. Add the yeast and unbeaten egg white; blend well.

Add the applesauce mixture and knead into a ball. Cover with plastic wrap and refrigerate overnight. Divide dough into four balls. Place on floured board and roll to 1/8 inch thickness with floured rolling pin. Fill, shape, brush with oil, and place on ungreased baking sheet.

KNISH FILLING

POTATO KNISH FILLING (P)

    3 large all-purpose potatoes, peeled and quartered
    3 tablespoons pareve margarine
    3 tablespoons canola oil
    3 large yellow onions, chopped
  1/4 cup fresh parsley, chopped
    2 large eggs, beaten
  1/2 teaspoon salt
  1/2 teaspoon freshly ground black pepper

Makes 48 cocktail-size.

Cook potatoes until tender and drain. Mash with potato masher until smooth. Melt butter or margarine and oil together; add onions and sauté until golden brown.

Add onions, parsley, eggs, salt, pepper to potatoes. Adjust seasonings to taste. Use with Crispy Dough. See "Knish Shapes" for baking time and temperature.

VEGETABLE KNISH FILLING (P)

    1 cup mashed potatoes, either fresh or instant
    1 tablespoon pareve margarine
    1 tablespoon canola oil
    1 large white onion, chopped
    1 cup carrots, shredded
    1 cup fresh button mushrooms, sliced
    1 cup zucchini, chopped
    2 large eggs or 4 egg whites, beaten
    1 tablespoon fresh parsley, chopped
  1/2 teaspoon salt
  1/2 teaspoon freshly ground black pepper

Makes 48 cocktail-size.

Continued on next page.

Cook potatoes until tender and drain. Mash with potato masher until smooth. Melt butter or margarine and oil together; add onion, carrots, mushrooms and zucchini and sauté until soft.

Drain liquid from vegetables and add with parsley, salt, pepper, and eggs to potatoes. Adjust seasonings to taste. Use with Crispy Dough. See "Knish Shapes" for baking time and temperature.

SWEET CHEESE KNISH FILLING (M)

1-1/2   pounds farmer cheese or
       large curd cottage cheese, drained
  1/4   cup dry bread crumbs
    2   large eggs, beaten
    1   tablespoon orange juice
  1/4   cup sugar

Makes 24 cocktail-size.

Combine all ingredients in food processor, using steel blade. Use with Sour Cream Dough. See "Knish Shapes" for baking time and temperature.

NOT SWEET CHEESE KNISH FILLING (M)

    8   ounces farmer cheese
  1/4   cup cream cheese, softened
  1/2   cup grated Swiss cheese
  2/3   cup feta cheese, finely crumbled
    2   large eggs, beaten
      pinch of pepper

Makes 24 cocktail-size.

Combine all ingredients in food processor, using steel blade. Season to taste with pepper. Use with Sour Cream Dough. See "Knish Shapes" for baking time and temperature.

KASHA KNISH FILLING (P)

2 cups all-purpose potatoes, peeled, cooked and drained
4 tablespoons canola oil
1/2 cup kasha (buckwheat groats or kernels)
2 large eggs, beaten
1 cup boiling water
2 medium white onions, chopped
4 tablespoons walnuts, chopped
1 teaspoon salt
1 teaspoon black pepper, freshly ground

Makes 12 large-size.

Cook potatoes until tender and drain. Mash with potato masher until smooth.

Heat skillet and add 2 tablespoons of oil. Add eggs and kasha and stir about 3 minutes, keeping grains separated. Add boiling water and cook on low heat about 15 minutes until all water is absorbed. Pour the other 2 tablespoons of oil into another skillet and sauté onions until they start to brown on edges. Sprinkle with salt and pepper.

Combine onions, potatoes, and nuts with prepared kasha and allow to cool. Adjust seasoning to taste. Use with any pareve knish dough. See "Knish Shapes" for baking time and temperature.

LIVER KNISH FILLING (F)

1 pound liver, either chicken or beef
1/4 cup canola oil
1 large yellow onion, chopped
2 large eggs, hard-boiled
    salt and pepper, to taste

Makes 30 cocktail-size.

Brown onion in hot oil and remove from heat.

Wash liver and broil until it is not pink inside, but do not overcook. Cut liver into chunks and chop to a coarse meal texture in food processor or meat grinder, using steel blade.

Add hard-boiled eggs, onions, salt, and pepper. Mix thoroughly. Use with Soft Dough. See "Knish Shapes" for baking time and temperature.

GROUND BEEF KNISH FILLING (F)

1-1/2 pounds lean ground beef
1/4 cup each green and red bell pepper, chopped
1 large white onion, chopped
1 tablespoon canola oil
1 egg, beaten
1 tablespoon Worcestershire sauce
1/2 teaspoon dry mustard
2 tablespoons ketchup
1/2 teaspoon salt
1/4 teaspoon pepper

Sauté bell peppers and onions in oil until soft in large frying pan. Pour into large mixing bowl.

Brown ground beef and add to vegetables. Stir in egg, Worcestershire sauce, mustard, ketchup, salt, and pepper.

Use with any pareve dough. See "Knish Shapes" for baking time and temperature.

PAREVE RICE KNISH FILLING (P)

1-1/2 cups brown or white rice, uncooked
3 cups water
1-1/2 teaspoons salt
4 tablespoons pareve margarine
4 teaspoons sugar
2 teaspoons cinnamon (optional)
2 large eggs, beaten
1 cup white raisins

Makes 15 large-size.

Wash rice, add water and bring to boil. Reduce to simmer and cook with salt and margarine for 20 minutes, until soft.

Add remaining ingredients and mix well. Use with Celia Elner's Dough. See "Knish Shapes" for baking time and temperature.

DAIRY RICE KNISH FILLING (M)

2-1/2 cups white or brown rice, uncooked
5 cups water
4 cups milk
1/2 cup sugar
1/4 pound margarine or butter
2 teaspoons cinnamon

Makes 24 large-size.

Wash rice, add water and bring to boil. Reduce to simmer, and cook for 15 minutes. Pour through sieve to drain excess water.

Add milk to rice, stir, and boil until very soft. Add sugar and cook mixture to the consistency of pudding. Remove from heat; add margarine or butter, stir, and allow to cool.

Place a mound of filling on knish dough. Shape (instructions below, brush with oil, and place on ungreased baking sheet and bake for 30 minutes. Use with any knish dough. See "Knish Shapes" for baking time and temperature.

SAUERKRAUT KNISH FILLING (P)

1 16-ounce can sauerkraut
3 tablespoons pareve margarine
1 large yellow onion
1 teaspoon sugar
   salt and freshly ground black pepper

Makes 24 cocktail-size.

Rinse sauerkraut under cold water; drain and pat dry with a paper towel. Chop sauerkraut in food processor and set aside.

Chop onion in food processor and sauté in margarine over low heat until soft. Add sauerkraut, sugar, salt, and pepper and stir thoroughly.

Cool before adding to pareve knish dough. See "Knish Shapes" for baking time and temperature.

PASSOVER KNISHES (P)

Dough:

  1   cup mashed potatoes
1/2   cup matzo meal
  2   tablespoons potato starch
  1   small yellow onion, finely chopped
  2   egg whites, beaten
1/4   teaspoon salt
1/2   teaspoon ground black pepper

Filling:

1/2   cup frozen chopped spinach
  1   cup button mushrooms

Preheat oven to 375°.

6 servings.

Continued on next page.

140

Combine dough ingredients and knead thoroughly. Divide the dough into 6 balls and flatten. Sauté mushrooms and add to spinach; stir thoroughly. Divide vegetable mixture into 6 portions and spread on dough.

Fold dough over vegetable and press edges together to seal. Place on baking sheet that has been sprayed with non-stick baking spray. Bake for 15 minutes, turn, and bake with topside down for another 15 minutes. Serve warm with sour cream for a dairy meal.

KNISH SIZES

Cocktail-size: Use 2 teaspoons of filling and a 3-inch cutter
Large-size: Use 1/3 to 1/2 cup of filling and a 4- or 5-inch cutter.

KNISH SHAPES

The shape of knishes is usually round or square. For the holiday or Purim, knishes are formed as triangles. The instructions below are for cocktail-size knishes. However, you may want to make yours much larger.

ROUND

Place ball of dough on floured board. Flatten with your hands to form a circle. Roll with floured rolling pin to 1/8 inch.

Cut dough with a 3-inch cutter. Place 2 teaspoons (or the size of a walnut) of filling mixture in center of circle. Fold edges over filling and pinch at the top to form round pastries.

Moisten dough at the top with a little water, if necessary, to make it stick together. Place on well-oiled baking sheet. Brush with oil or egg wash* and bake at 375° for 15 or 20 minutes or until golden brown.

SQUARE

Place ball of dough on a floured board. Flatten with your hands and cut to form a rectangle. Roll with a floured rolling pin to 1/8 inch.

Cut into long rectangle about 4 inches wide. Starting 1 inch from the long edge, place a 2 inch wide by 1 inch high strip of filling on dough.

Fold ends over filling. Stretch front portion of dough over filling and then overlap back portion of dough over. Trim excess dough and use later. Cut between mounds make squares.

Place on well-oiled baking sheet. Brush with oil or egg wash* and bake at 375° for 15 to 20 minutes or until golden brown.

*Egg Wash: Beat 1 egg yolk with 1 teaspoon of water or use 1 beaten egg white.

.

OTHER TASTY DISHES

HORS D'OEUVRES
AND APPETIZERS
Also see Kreplach, p. 162

STUFFED MUSHROOMS (M)

24 large fresh button mushrooms
1/4 cup plus 2 tablespoons butter
1/4 cup scallions, chopped
 1 clove garlic, minced
1/4 cup plus 2 tablespoons butter
1/2 cup Cheddar cheese, grated
2/3 cup dry breadcrumbs
 1 tablespoon dried chopped parsley
 2 tablespoons dry white wine

Preheat oven to 425°.   24 servings.

Wash and drain mushrooms and remove stems, reserving caps.
Chop enough stems to make 1 cup.

In medium saucepan, sauté stems, scallion, and garlic in 1/4
cup butter until tender. Stir in parsley, breadcrumbs and
cheese.
Spoon crumb mixture into mushroom caps.

Combine 2 tablespoons melted butter and wine and pour into
bottom of a 9" x 13" baking pan. Arrange mushrooms in pan
and bake uncovered for 15 to 20 minutes or until heated
through.

RUMAKI WITH LIVER OR DATES (F)

12 chicken livers (12 to 14 ounces)
OR
24 small dates
1/2 can sliced water chestnuts (24 pieces)
12 slices beef frye

Marinade for chicken livers:

1/4 cup apricot all fruit spread
1/4 cup soy sauce
 2 tablespoons canola oil
1/4 cup water
 1 tablespoon sugar
1/4 teaspoon garlic powder
1/8 teaspoon ground ginger

24 servings.

Combine all-fruit spread, soy sauce, oil, water, sugar, garlic powder, and ginger. Add water chestnuts.

Cut chicken livers in half and add to all-fruit spread mixture. Do not marinade dates. Cover and chill 4 hours or overnight.

Broil beef frye for 3 minutes, 4 inches from broiler element.

Wrap 1/2 slice of beef frye around a liver half or date, and a water chestnut slice. Secure with a wooden toothpick.

Broil for 8 minutes until livers are no longer pink; turn once. Serve warm.

SWEET AND SOUR MEATBALLS (F)

4 slices bread, wheat, white, sourdough, or hallah
2 pounds ground beef
1 clove garlic
2 large eggs, beaten
2 small carrots
1 medium white onion
  salt and pepper, to taste

48 servings.

Moisten and squeeze bread. Place bread, garlic, eggs, carrots, onion, salt, and pepper in blender or food processor with steel blade; blend until smooth.

Add beef to mixture. Shape into 1-inch meatballs. Place on baking sheet and broil until lightly brown.

Sauce:

1 bottle hot ketchup plus 1 ketchup bottleful of water
1 8-ounce can crushed pineapple, in own juice, not drained

Combine ingredients, place meatballs into mixture, and simmer for 1 hour. Serve with toothpicks.

SPINACH AND ARTICHOKE DIP (M)

1 large can artichokes in water, drained
1 cup chopped spinach, cooked and drained
2 cups light mayonnaise
2 cups grated Parmesan cheese
  paprika for sprinkling

Combine all ingredients and mix well.

Pour into greased casserole dish sprayed with baking spray. Sprinkle with paprika. Bake for 20 minutes until browned. Serve with chips or crackers.

DOGS IN A BLANKET (F)

Dough:

2-1/2 cups flour, unbleached and presifted
  1/4 teaspoon salt
  3/4 cup pareve margarine
    6 tablespoons ice water
    2 1-pound packages kosher cocktail-size hot dogs
    1 egg, beaten

Preheat oven to 350°.   Makes 48.

Combine salt and flour, and add margarine. Blend with a pastry cutter until mixture is like coarse meal.

Add ice water and knead with your hands to form into a ball. (Add a little more water if dough is too crumbly, one tablespoon at a time.)

Divide in half. Lightly flour each ball of dough and wrap in plastic wrap. Refrigerate 1 hour or overnight..

Turn onto lightly floured board and knead until smooth. With floured rolling pin, roll out to 1/4 inch thickness.

Cut into pieces large enough to cover cocktail-size hot dogs. Wrap hot dogs with dough and pinch to close. Place on ungreased baking sheet and brush with beaten egg. Bake for 15 minutes or until golden brown.

Variation:

Wrap hot dogs in commercial brand crescent roll dough halves. Do not brush tops with anything and bake until browned.

GEFILTE FISH

Many years ago, rabbinical Jewish authorities determined that removing bones from a fish in a certain way was work. Since no work may be done on the Sabbath, people started making fish that was boned and gefilte fish became popular. Because eating fish is a token of wisdom, fortune, and fertility, gefilte fish is frequently served during holidays and at celebration meals. It is often seen in Polish restaurants where it is listed on the menus as "fish, Jewish style." The Yiddish translation is "stuffed fish" or "fish cakes."

Carp and whitefish are often used in recipes, but almost any fish can be used. Gefilte fish is formed into balls or ovals and usually served cold for hors d'oeuvres or as an appetizer. A lettuce leaf and a cooked carrot slice will often garnish the plate. Ground horseradish that is colored with beet juice, known as red horseradish, usually accompanies this delicacy. Some people serve gefilte fish with the jellied stock, but most people do not like it.

Gefilte fish can be found in the ethnic food section in many grocery stores throughout North America. Better yet, try the Slow Gefilte Fish recipe or use the recipe below.

FAST GEFILTE FISH (P)

16 pieces jarred gefilte fish, any brand
 1 large white onion, cut in chunks
 5 medium carrots, sliced thin
 4 stalks celery, diced
 1 tablespoon paprika
 1 teaspoon freshly ground black pepper

Drain jellied stock from jar and pour into a pot. Add onion, carrot, celery, pepper, and paprika. Cover and bring to a boil. Simmer for 10-15 minutes, until vegetables are soft.

Place gefilte fish patties in a 9" x 13" baking pan and cover with stock mixture. Cover with foil and bake for 15 minutes. Turn patties, cover pan again, and continue baking for another 15 minutes. Serve warm or chilled with horseradish.

SLOW GEFILTE FISH (P)

1-1/2 pounds cod fillets
1-1/2 pounds red snapper fillets
   2 medium white onions
   2 large carrots
   3 large eggs, beaten
1-1/2 teaspoons salt
  3/4 teaspoon freshly ground black pepper
  3/4 teaspoon sugar
  3/4 cup matzo meal

Makes 12 large oval-shaped patties or 36 cocktail-size pieces.

In a food processor chop fish, carrots, and onions with steel blade. Add egg, salt, pepper, sugar, and matzo meal; process until smooth. With wet hands, form mixture into either golf ball-size pieces, or into fat oval-shaped patties.

Gefilte fish broth:

   8 cups water
   4 stalks celery
   2 large white onions
   3 large carrots
   3 pareve (vegetable) bouillon cubes
  1/2 tablespoon freshly ground black pepper
   1 tablespoon sugar

Place broth ingredients into a large, deep pot and cover. Bring to a boil and then reduce to a simmer. Stir to dissolve bouillon cubes.

Gently slide the formed fish into water with a spoon. Cook slowly for 1 hour if cocktail-size or two hours for larger pieces, occasionally turning fish. Allow patties to cool in pot, then carefully remove with a slotted spoon.

To make jellied broth, strain vegetables, and loose pieces of fish from broth. Add one package of unflavored kosher gelatin and chill to jell. Serve warm or chilled fish with red horseradish, and a carrot slice from broth.

CHOPPED HERRING (P)

1 small jar of herring fillets, in wine sauce
2 large eggs, hard-boiled
1 tart apple, pared and grated
3 tablespoons dry breadcrumbs

Drain the herring but save the onions from the jar. Chop herring and onions with eggs to a coarse consistency. Add grated apple and bread crumbs. Stir thoroughly and chill. Serve with bagel chips, crackers, or party breads.

RED HERRING (M)

2 12-ounce jars herring fillets, in wine sauce
1 16-ounce can whole cranberry sauce
1 small yellow onion, sliced
8 ounces plain yogurt

About 30 pieces.

Drain herring but keep the onions from jar. Beat yogurt and cranberry sauce until blended; add sliced onion. Stir thoroughly and chill overnight. Remove herring fillets with a fork and set on decorative dish to serve. Garnish with onions and cranberries.

PICKLED HERRING (P)

2 large herrings	1 tablespoon brown sugar
1 large yellow onion, sliced	3 bay leaves
1 cup white vinegar	1 tablespoon pickling spice
1/4 cup water	1 small lemon, thinly sliced

Remove head and tail from gutted fish. Place fish in a glass jar and add cold water to cover. Refrigerate, for 8 hours. Wash herring thoroughly under cold running water; remove fins and scales. Remove skin or not. Place whole herrings or sections in a 1-quart jar. Add onion. In saucepot, bring vinegar, water, and sugar to a boil. Add liquid to jar with bay leaves, spice, and lemon slices. Cover and refrigerate for 24 hours before serving.

REAL CHOPPED LIVER (F)

Chopped liver can be served on crackers, party-size rye, or black bread as hors d'oeuvres. It can also be served over lettuce as an appetizer, with some chopped hard-boiled egg, sprinkled on top for garnish. It is also great as a sandwich with onion slices and tomato on Jewish rye bread.

    1   pound liver, either chicken or beef
    2   tablespoons canola oil
    1   large yellow onion, chopped
    2   large eggs, hard-boiled
    1/2 cup light mayonnaise
        salt and pepper, to taste

Wash liver and broil until it is not pink inside, but do not overcook. Cut liver into chunks and chop, using steel blade in food processor, to a coarse texture.

Brown onion in hot oil and remove from heat. Add liver, hard-boiled eggs, onions, mayonnaise, salt, and pepper and process until well mixed. Serve chilled with crackers or matzo.

MOCK CHOPPED LIVER (P)

    1   cup brown lentils
    3   cups water
    1   8-ounce can peas, well drained
    3   medium yellow onions, chopped
    2   tablespoons extra virgin olive oil
    2   teaspoons garlic, minced
    7   eggs, hard-boiled
    1/2 cup pecans, finely chopped
    1/2 cup unsalted peanuts, finely chopped
    1/2 cup walnuts, finely chopped
    2   teaspoons salt
    1/2 teaspoon pepper

Makes 6 cups.

Continued on next page.

154

Soak lentils for about 3 hours in 3 cups of water. Boil for 1 hour or until all water is absorbed. Sauté onions and garlic in oil until light brown.

Discard 3 of the egg yolks (use 4 whole eggs and 3 egg whites). In food processor fitted with steel blade, add remaining ingredients with eggs, lentils, onions, and garlic. Chop until smooth. Serve chilled with bagel chips or matzo.

CHEESE PINWHEELS (M)

Filling:

- 1 pound farmer cheese
- 4 tablespoons butter or margarine
- 1 cup chopped scallions
- 1 large egg, beaten
- 2 tablespoons chopped parsley
- 2 tablespoons sour cream
   salt and pepper, to taste

48 cocktail-size appetizers.

Grate farmer cheese in food processor until smooth. Melt butter or margarine; add scallions and sauté until limp but not brown. Add to cheese with egg, parsley, sour cream, salt, and pepper.

Dough:

See Sour Cream Dough, p. 133.

Place ball of dough on a floured board. Flatten with your hands and cut into a rectangle. Roll with floured rolling pin to 1/8 inch thickness and about 12 inches long by 7 inches wide.

Spread with filling, leaving a 1/2-inch border. Roll from long edge like a jellyroll to about 2 inches in diameter; cut into 1-inch slices. Lay the pieces on their sides on a lightly greased baking sheet. Refrigerate for at least 1/2 hour or overnight. Bake for 30 minutes, or until golden brown.

FALAFEL (P)

Falafel is very popular in Israel. It is thought of as the "all-Israeli" food, just as hot dogs are "all-American." Vendors can be found everywhere on the streets in Israel, like hot dog vendors in some big cities in America. At their outdoor stands, which are called kiosks, they also offer fresh, colorful salads and vegetables that are used for toppings. Jewish Yemenites brought falafel to Israel but this delicacy is probably Arabic in origin. Want some good falafel here in the U.S.A.? Make the recipe below or go to New York City!

  2/3 cup bulgur wheat
    2 15-ounce cans chick-peas (garbanzo beans)
    4 cloves garlic, peeled and coarsely chopped
    2 large eggs, beaten
    2 tablespoons lemon juice
    4 tablespoons fresh parsley, finely chopped
    2 teaspoons ground cumin
  1/2 teaspoon ground paprika
  1/2 teaspoon ground coriander
  1/2 teaspoon dried basil
  1/2 teaspoon dried marjoram
1-1/2 teaspoons salt
  1/4 teaspoon ground cayenne or black pepper
1-1/2 cups fresh bread crumbs (pita bread crumbs will do)
      canola oil for frying

Makes 40 Falafel balls.

Pour bulgur wheat into a sieve; place in a container of warm water to cover bulgur for 20 minutes and drain. Press out excess water by pressing with a paper towel.

In food processor that has been fitted with steel blade, pulse process bulgur and chickpeas until chickpeas are chopped, but not puréed. Pour chickpea mixture into a mixing bowl, and add garlic, lemon juice, eggs, herbs, and seasonings. Stir well and add enough breadcrumbs to make mixture hold together.

Continued on next page.

Knead well with your hands. Cover and place in refrigerator for 30 minutes or refrigerate for up to 2 days. Press 1 tablespoon of mixture in palms of your hands and roll into a ball and then flatten slightly.

Carefully slide about 1/4 of the balls into hot oil to deep-fry. Fry for 2 minutes until browned and crisp on all sides. Repeat until all of the mixture is used. Drain on paper towels.

Serve with pita bread, Hummus (p. 158), Tahini Dip (p. 159), fresh vegetables, Cucumber, Tomato, Bell Pepper Salad (p. 191), Tabouleh (p. 157), and either Eggplant Salad (p. 192) or Baba Ganoush (p. 158).

To make a sandwich, place several falafel balls in a pita bread pocket. Top with Tahini Dip and any, or all, of the above vegetable mixtures.

TABOULEH (P)

3/4 cup bulgur
  3 plum tomatoes
1/2 cup fresh chopped parsley
1/2 cup chopped scallions
1/4 cup extra virgin olive oil
1/4 cup fresh lemon juice
1/2 teaspoon salt
  1 tablespoon dried mint, crumbled

Makes 4 cups.

Pour bulgur into a sieve. Dip filled sieve into warm water until bulgur is covered. Allow to soak for 30 minutes. Lift sieve and squeeze out excess water. Pour into mixing bowl.

Add remaining ingredients and mix thoroughly. Cover and refrigerate overnight. Stir salad during refrigeration period and just before serving. Bulgur will soften and the flavors of the salad will blend together. Serve with pita bread that has been cut into triangles.

HUMMUS (P)

1 15-ounce can prepared chickpeas (garbanzo beans),
     drained; reserve 3 tablespoons liquid
1/4 cup tahini (sesame paste), well stirred
2 tablespoons fresh lemon juice
3 tablespoons extra virgin olive oil
3 cloves garlic, minced
    pinch of salt and freshly ground white pepper

Makes 2 cups.

In food processor combine chickpeas, tahini, lemon juice, garlic, salt and pepper, oil, and reserved chickpea liquid. Blend to a pastelike consistency. Add water, one tablespoon at a time, if necessary.

Pour into serving dish and refrigerate for several hours for flavors to blend.

Garnish with parsley sprigs, sun dried tomatoes, sliced, and pitted ripe (black) olives, and 1 tablespoon lightly toasted pignoli (pine) nuts. Chill overnight to allow flavors to blend. Serve at room temperature with pita bread that has been cut into triangles for dipping.

BABA GANOUSH (P)

2 medium-sized eggplants (about 1 pound each)
2 cloves garlic, finely minced
1/3 cup tahini (sesame paste)
2-1/2 tablespoons fresh lemon juice
2 tablespoons cold water
1 tablespoon extra virgin olive oil
2 tablespoons fresh parsley leaves, finely chopped
1/2 teaspoon salt
1/8 teaspoon black pepper, freshly ground
    pinch of cayenne pepper

Makes 2 cups.

Continued on next page.

Pierce eggplants with a fork several times to avoid eggplants from exploding during broiling. Place on foil-lined baking sheet, 6 inches below broiler element. Broil eggplants, turning often, until the skin is blistered and charred, and the pulp is soft, about 25 minutes.

Cut eggplants in half and allow to cool. Remove remaining skin and stem, and discard.

Place pulp in food processor that has been fitted with the steel blade and process until finely chopped.

Thoroughly stir tahini and add to eggplant. Add remaining ingredients. Pulse-process until almost smooth, but not puréed.

Pour baba ganoush into serving bowl, cover, and refrigerate. Serve with falafel or pita bread cut into triangles.

TAHINI DIP (P)

    1/2 cup tahini (sesame paste)
    1/2 cup water
    1/4 teaspoon salt
    2-1/2 tablespoons lemon juice
       3 cloves of garlic, crushed
          pinch of white pepper

Makes 1 cup.

Stir tahini until well mixed. Combine with water, salt, lemon juice, garlic, and pepper and mix thoroughly. Add more water if a thinner consistency is desired.

Garnish with paprika and fresh parsley. Serve with pita bread that has been cut into triangles for dipping.

SOUP

Mother knows best!

Chicken soup has been referred to as "Jewish Penicillin" for generations. A few years ago, scientists finally decided to check it out. They found there really is something in chicken soup that makes it very effective in helping to relieve symptoms of colds and flu.

MOTHER'S CHICKEN SOUP (F)

- 1 pound chicken breasts, skinned and boned
- 1 pound chicken thighs, skinned and boned
- 1 whole yellow onion
- 3 stalks celery, with leaves
- 3 large carrots, brushed
- 2 tablespoons cilantro (Italian parsley), finely chopped
- 1 tablespoon salt
- 1/2 teaspoon ground white pepper

Fill a 1-gallon pot halfway with water; add chicken. Bring water to a boil and "skim the scum," as my mother would say, with a spoon.

Cut washed and brushed carrots into 1-inch chunks. Thoroughly wash celery and break each stalk in half. Reduce heat to simmer and place vegetables, cilantro, salt, and pepper into pot. Cover pot and continue to cook for 2-1/2 hours.

Place a colander over a large container and pour soup into it to strain. If desired, discard onions and celery. Pour chicken, carrots, and broth back into pot.

Cook kreplach, mandlen, noodles, or matzo balls in separate pot so they will not absorb the liquid from soup. Add to soup before serving.

AWARD WINNING CHICKEN SOUP RECIPE (F)

See Award Winning Kugel recipe, p. 72.

1 3-pound chicken, cut in quarters
2 carrots, sliced
1 large yellow onion, sliced
2 stalks of celery with leaves, sliced
1 large parsnip, sliced
1 tablespoon chopped parsley, dried or fresh
1 teaspoon dill, dried or fresh
1 kosher chicken bouillon cube
1 kosher beef bouillon cube

Remove skin from chicken. Place chicken into a pressure cooker or large pot. Add carrots, onion, celery, parsnip, parsley, dill, and bouillon cubes. Cover with water and cook until vegetables are soft. If you are using a pressure cooker, this takes about 15 minutes.

Drain broth into another pot. Remove chicken and debone. Place cooked vegetables and 1 cup of soup into a blender or food processor with steel blade. Blend until pureed. Add soup and heat. Serve with crackers and boiled chicken.

MANDLEN (P)

2 large eggs, beaten
1 tablespoon canola oil
1 cup flour, unbleached and presifted
1/4 teaspoon salt
1/2 teaspoon baking powder

Preheat oven to 375°.

Beat together eggs and oil. Slowly add to flour and knead until smooth. Roll to 1/4 inch thickness and cut into 1/2-inch pieces. Place on greased baking sheet and bake 15 minutes.

KREPLACH (F)

There are foods that are similar in many cultures, and kreplach is one of them. This filled noodle, that is popular in Ashkenazic Jewish cuisine, is believed to have been adapted from the Chinese won ton or Italian ravioli. The Polish version is a pirogi. When stuffed with chicken, it is often used in soup. Some people prefer to fry it and serve it with gravy. There are variations stuffed with cheese and served sprinkled with cinnamon and sugar. This treat is often served for the holiday of Purim since its shape is triangular, like Haman's hat. It is also a traditional food the night before Yom Kippur and on Hoshanah Rabbah (the 7th day of Sukkot).

```
    1   tablespoon canola oil
    1   small yellow onion, chopped
1-1/2   cups chicken, cooked and shredded
    1   large egg, beaten
    1   tablespoon chopped parsley
        salt and pepper, to taste
        Homemade Noodle Dough (p. 38)
        OR commercially made won ton wraps
```

Lightly brown the onion in oil. Finely grind chicken in food processor. Add onions, beaten egg, parsley, and salt and pepper.

Prepare dough and divide into two balls. Cover with a moist towel. Roll out half of the dough to 1/8" thickness with a floured rolling pin, or hand flatten and run through a pasta machine. Follow directions in Homemade Noodle Dough recipe.

When dough is until dough is thin and easy to handle, cut into strips that are 2 inches wide. Put 1/2 teaspoon mounds of filling about 2 inches apart and cut into 2-inch squares. Fold each square into a triangle and press edges together. Wet inside edges if necessary to make them stick.

Gently place kreplach into boiling water and cook 10 minutes. Uncooked kreplach can be covered and refrigerated for one day or frozen. Serve in chicken soup or as an appetizer with sweet and sour sauce.

MATZO BALLS (KNAIDLACH) (P OR F)

1 cup matzo meal
1/3 cup Passover oil
1/2 cup water or club soda*

4 large eggs, beaten
1 teaspoon salt
dash ground black pepper

Beat eggs and add water, oil, salt, and pepper. Mix well. Add matzo meal and stir thoroughly. Refrigerate 1 hour.

Form into 1-1/2-inch balls and gently drop into boiling water with a spatula or large spoon. Cook 20 minutes. Remove with slotted spoon and add to soup.

Variations:

Add one of the following:

1/4 teaspoon each ground ginger and ground cinnamon.

OR 2 tablespoons finely chopped parsley, 2 tablespoons chopped onion, 1/4 teaspoon each garlic powder and cayenne.

OR 1 tablespoon finely chopped nuts plus a dash ground ginger.

OR 1 cup of mashed potatoes.

Add "soul," by combining:

2 tablespoons matzo meal
2 tablespoons hot fat
1 egg
    dash salt

Tuck a small ball of this mixture in the center of each knaidle dumpling,

OR put chopped liver or slivered almonds in the center.

* For heavier matzo balls, use 1/2 cup chicken soup.

HOT CABBAGE BORSCHT (F)

2-1/2 pounds beef cubes
2 quarts boiling water
2 pounds cabbage
1 large yellow onion
1/2 cup lemon juice
4 tablespoons brown sugar
1 28-ounce can stewed tomatoes
1 cup dried lima beans or 1 medium can, drained
salt, to taste

6 servings.

Soak lima beans overnight in water, or use drained canned limas. Cover beef cubes with water and bring to boil. Turn heat to simmer and, with a spoon, skim the scum that will form on top of water.

Cut onion and cabbage into chunks and add to broth. Add lemon juice, salt, brown sugar, lima beans and stewed tomatoes. Cover pot and cook 2 hours or until lima beans and meat are tender.

COLD RED BEET BORSCHT (P)

9 red beets (each about 2 inches in diameter)
1 medium yellow onion, cut in half
6 cups water
1/2 teaspoon salt
1 tablespoon sugar
2 tablespoons lemon juice

Wash and scrub beets with a vegetable brush. Combine beets, onion, and water in a medium-size heavy pot and bring to boil. Cover and simmer over low heat for about 1 hour or until beets are tender; drain, saving liquid except for the last few tablespoons, which may be sandy. Wash the pot and, slowly pour liquid back into pot.

Continued on next page.

Coarsely grate the beets and add to liquid with salt and sugar. Cook for 2 minutes, stirring over low heat. Remove from heat and add lemon juice. Taste and adjust seasoning. Soup should be slightly sweet and sour. Chill and serve with sour cream, chunks of cold potato, diced cucumber, and/or diced hard-boiled egg.

SCHAV (M)

This is a tart soup. The bitter sorrel leaves make it a perfect food to eat during Passover since we are supposed to eat bitter herbs.

1/2	pound fresh sorrel, turnip greens, or mustard greens
1/2	pound fresh spinach
6	chopped scallions, divided
1	small yellow onion, finely chopped
2	tablespoons unsalted butter or margarine
2	tablespoons fresh dill; reserve 1 teaspoon
2	tablespoons fresh basil; reserve 1 teaspoon
2	tablespoons fresh parsley; reserve 1 teaspoon
4	cups vegetable broth
1/4	cup white wine
1	cup half-and-half cream or whole milk
1/2	cup sour cream or yogurt
2	hard-boiled eggs, chopped
1	cucumber, peeled, seeded and diced
	salt and freshly ground black pepper, to taste

6 servings.

Thoroughly wash sorrel and spinach and chop stems. In a large, heavy pot, sauté the onion and scallions in butter. Add the sorrel and spinach leaves and stems.

Cook covered for a few minutes with most of the basil, dill, and parsley. Add vegetable broth and wine and bring to a boil. Reduce heat and simmer for 10 minutes, uncovered. Add the cream or milk, sour cream, salt, and pepper, and heat briefly. Purée in a food processor. Serve hot or cold. Garnish with the reserved herbs, hard boiled eggs, cucumber, and, a dollop of sour cream.

MUSHROOM AND BARLEY SOUP (P)

1/2 cup small dried lima beans or 1 small can, drained
1 tablespoon canola oil
2 medium yellow onions, thinly sliced
2 garlic cloves, minced
1/2 pound fresh button mushrooms, quartered
4 ounces fresh portabella mushrooms, sliced and halved
4 ounces fresh Italian mushrooms, quartered
1 cup celery, finely chopped
1 cup carrots, finely chopped
7 cups boiling water
1/4 cup soy sauce
1/2 cup raw pearl barley
1 extra large vegetable bouillon cube
1/4 teaspoon freshly ground black pepper
1 tablespoon fresh dill, chopped
1/3 cup dry sherry or 2 teaspoons honey

6 servings.

Soak lima beans overnight or use canned limas; drain. Wash barley in a strainer.

Slice onions, mushrooms, celery, and carrots in food processor. Warm oil in soup pot on low heat. Add sliced vegetables and garlic and sauté for about 5 minutes.

Add water, soy sauce, barley, lima beans, bouillon, pepper, dill, and optional sherry or honey to pot of sautéed veggies. Increase heat to high, and bring to a boil. Cover pot and reduce heat to simmer. Cook for 45 minutes.

Adjust seasonings to taste. Flavors will blend overnight. If soup becomes too thick, add water.

SPLIT PEA SOUP (F)

2 pounds lean stew meat
3 quarts water
2 tablespoons salt
1 pound dried split peas
1/2 cup raw pearl barley
2 large yellow onions, chopped
6 large carrots, sliced into chunks
   garlic powder and pepper, to taste

In a 6-quart pot, boil meat, and salt in water. Skim the scum that will form on top of water with a spoon and discard.

Wash the split-peas in a strainer; soak in cold water to cover for 30 minutes. Wash barley in strainer. Add split-peas and barley to meat. Cover and simmer for 1 hour, stirring occasionally. Add onions and carrots. Continue to cook for 1 more hour, stirring occasionally.

BREAD

 ## HALLAH

Two long braided hallot are traditionally served at the Friday night Sabbath meal. The two loaves represent the double portion of manna (small seeds from tamarisk trees) that was collected by the Israelites for the Sabbath every Friday while wandering in the desert after leaving Egypt. The biblical recollection tells that "a layer of golden dew fell on the desert floor. A second layer of dew fell and encased the manna in a dome of shimmering silver." An embroidered cloth simulating the second layer is supposed to cover the Sabbath hallah.

The number two also represents the two covered stacks of Showbreads that were offered to the kohanim (priests) of the Holy Temple. It is said that the Showbreads were kept out for one week and were closely guarded. One week later, they were replaced. The replaced batch was miraculously as fresh as it was on the day it was baked.

The Torah says that a small piece of the dough from each large batch of bread must be separated and "offered" to the kohanim. Therefore an observant baker will take a 1- or 2-inch ball of the unbaked dough and burn it, or place it in a napkin and throw it away. When this is done, a special prayer is said. On the Sabbath, another prayer, called the Hamotzi, is said over the bread. The translation says that we thank God for giving us "bread from the earth." The wheat that we use to make the bread is actually from the earth and, in the prayer, we are thanking God for giving us the wisdom that enables us to make it. Afterwards, the bread is broken, not cut, and tasted. A knife is not used because it may suggest images of violence.

People form the dough into many symbolic shapes depending on the celebration or their regional custom. The letter "shin," a star, a dreidle, or animal shapes are sometimes used. For the holiday of Rosh Hashanah, the bread is usually formed into a circular shape to symbolize a long span of life and a well rounded year. The spiral would be higher in the center and it represents "the ascent to heaven." Sometimes a ladder is formed at the top of the bread to depict the ascent, or a crown is placed on top to glorify God. For the holiday of Purim, some people fashion their hallah in a triangular shape.

This ancient bread is full of symbolism that goes beyond what I have written. If you are interested in learning more about this interesting bread, see The Jewish Book of Why or The Jewish Catalog.

ḤALLAḤ (P)

```
   1  1/4-ounce package active dry yeast
 1/4  cup sugar
1-1/2  cups warm water, 120° to 130° Fahrenheit
   3  whole eggs, beaten
   5  cups bread flour, divided
1-1/2  teaspoons salt
 1/2  cup applesauce
   1  egg white, beaten
      poppy seeds for sprinkling (optional)
```

Preheat oven to 375°.   Makes 2 loaves.

In large bowl dissolve yeast with 1 teaspoon of the sugar in 1/4 cup of the water until foamy to proof. Add whole eggs, remainder of the water, remainder of the sugar, and 2-1/2 cups flour to yeast mixture. Beat for 10 minutes with dough hooks on electric beater. Cover with a damp towel and let rise in a warm place for 1 hour. Add salt, applesauce, and remaining 2-1/2 cups flour. Mix until dough comes clean from bowl.

Turn onto floured board and knead for 10 minutes, sprinkling with flour as necessary to make a soft, malleable dough. Cover with dry towel and let rise for 1 hour. Punch down, cover, and allow dough to rise for 30 minutes. Punch down again and divide into two portions. Divide each portion into three long strips to braid; or fashion into long strip and form into spiral shape, with center higher than outside. Place on greased baking sheet. Cover and let rise for 30 minutes. Brush with beaten egg white. Sprinkle with optional poppy seeds. Bake for 40 minutes or until browned all around.

BAGELS

Lox without bagels? Impossible!

Bagels are absolutely a must with lox (in my opinion). However, everyone seems to have their own favorite way to eat the popular bagel and lox sandwich. I like to prepare it open faced on a toasted sesame seed bagel that has been spread with some cream cheese (not too thick), about one ounce of nova lox on each half, and topped with slices of cucumber, tomato, and onion. Sometimes I will add a slice of Muenster or American cheese or a little bit of another smoked fish. If I order bagels and lox at a delicatessen, I usually have to disassemble it, scrape away most of the half pound of cream cheese that is usually placed on the bagel, and re-stack everything, my way!

The tradition of eating a Sunday breakfast or brunch meal that includes smoked fish and bagels, and frequently kugel, has been around since at least the 1940's in America. It probably came with the Jewish immigrants when they brought bagels to this country.

The word "bagel" is Yiddish for "roll." The art of bagel baking was brought New York from Russia or Poland around 1900. The flavored varieties, like pumpernickel, garlic, rye, and egg, are American. Until the last 15 years or less, bagels were almost totally unknown by non-Jews who did not live near the big cities, like New York, Philadelphia, and Chicago, or in southeastern Florida, and some parts of California.

According to Leah W. Leonard, who wrote Jewish Cookery, published in 1949, the art of bagel baking was almost lost in the United States. "Older men in the industry fear that bagels will disappear because the younger bakers show no enthusiasm for learning the method. A machine for mixing and forming bagels, much like the machinery for turning out doughnuts, has not as yet proved successful. Handmade bagels are still baked and sold by almost all Jewish bakeries." Today, however, bagels can be found in almost every city in this country, thanks to a famous fast-food chain that started serving breakfast bagels years ago, and modern machinery.

This chewy, doughnut-shaped bread, that is crusty on the outside and soft on the inside, can be purchased fresh and hot straight from the oven, usually in the morning, at one of the many bagel bakeries that have sprung up across the country. Bagels that can also be purchased at major food markets in the frozen food section or bakery department, but they usually do not compare to the bagel bakery or Jewish delicatessen varieties. The very best bagels are prepared with this recipe.

BAGELS (P)

4 cups white bread flour
1 1/4-ounce package active dry yeast
1-1/2 cups warm water, 120° to 130° Fahrenheit
1/4 cup sugar
1 teaspoon salt

Preheat oven to 350°.   Makes 12.

Proof yeast in 1/4 cup of the water mixed with 1 teaspoon of the sugar. Let sit for 10 minutes until foamy. Combine with 2 cups of the flour, 3 tablespoons of the sugar, and salt.

Beat with an electric mixer on low speed for 30 seconds, scraping bowl constantly. Beat on high speed for 3 minutes.

Stir in, with a spoon, as much of remaining flour as you can. Turn out onto a lightly floured surface. Knead in enough remaining flour to make a moderately stiff dough that is smooth and elastic. Cover with a towel and allow to sit for 10 minutes.

Quickly divide dough into 12 portions. Shape each portion into a smooth ball. Punch a hole in the center of each ball with a floured finger. Pull dough gently to make about a 2-inch hole, keeping bagel uniformly shaped. Place on greased baking sheet. Cover and allow to rise for 15 minutes.

Continued on next page.

171

Bring 7 cups of water with remaining sugar to a boil in a 4-1/2 quart Dutch oven. Reduce heat to simmer so water will be ready when you need it (after the next step).

Broil raised bagels about 5 inches under broiler element in oven for 2 minutes. Turn bagels and broil for another 2 minutes, tops should not be browned.

Simmer bagels in water, 4 at a time, for 4 minutes. Turn and simmer for 3 more minutes. Drain well on paper towels. Place bagels on greased baking sheet. Bake for 15 minutes and turn. Bake for 15 more minutes until browned.

PHYLLIS'S PASSOVER POPOVERS (P)

1 cup matzo meal
2/3 cup water
1/3 cup oil
1/4 teaspoon salt
1 tablespoon sugar
3 large eggs, beaten

Preheat oven to 350°.   Makes 12.

Heat water, and oil in a medium saucepan and bring to a boil. Remove from heat.

Add matzo meal, sugar, and salt; mix well. Return pan to low heat and cook, stirring, for 1 minute. Remove from heat and cool about 5 minutes; add 1 beaten egg. When mixture is completely smooth, beat in a second egg. Continue adding eggs one at a time, beating thoroughly after each addition.

Grease a muffin pan and fill each opening half-way with batter. Bake 55-60 minutes or until golden brown and firm.

DARK RYE BREAD (P)

3 cups rye flour
1 cup whole wheat flour
2 cups white flour, unbleached and presifted
1/4 cup cocoa
1-1/2 teaspoons salt
1 tablespoon caraway seeds (optional)
2 1/4-ounce packages active dry yeast
1/2 cup warm water, 120° to 130° Fahrenheit
2 teaspoons white sugar
1/2 cup honey
1-1/2 cups water, room temperature
3 tablespoons canola oil
1 egg white, beaten
cornmeal for sprinkling pan

Preheat oven to 375°.   Makes 2 loaves.

Dissolve yeast in the 1/2 cup warm water with white sugar and let sit for 10 minutes until it foams. Sift together flours, cocoa, and salt; add optional caraway seeds, oil and yeast mixture and mix with electric beater.

In a saucepan, warm 1/2 cup honey with the 1-1/2 cups water and stir to mix well; slowly add to flour mixture and continue to mix until thoroughly combined.

Knead dough until it does not stick to sides of bowl and is smooth and elastic. Place on floured surface and knead 5 minutes more. Place on greased baking sheet and cover with a damp towel. Let dough rise in unheated oven over pan of warm water for about 1 hour.

Remove from oven, punch down, and knead on lightly floured surface. Divide dough into two portions and let rest for 10 minutes. Shape into 2 long oval loaves. Sprinkle 2 greased baking sheets with cornmeal and place loaves on top. Cover with dry towel and let rise for 30 minutes.

Brush dough with egg white. Bake for 45 minutes. Brush bread again and bake for 5 minutes longer or until browned on all sides.

JEWISH RYE BREAD (P)

1 1/4-ounce package active dry yeast
2-1/2 tablespoons sugar
1 cup plus 2 tablespoons warm water, 120° to 130° F.
2-1/4 cups white bread flour, divided
3/4 cups rye flour
1 tablespoon cornmeal
2 teaspoons caraway seeds
1-1/4 teaspoons salt
1 tablespoon oil
1 egg white, beaten

Preheat oven to 375°.   Makes 1 large loaf.

Place ingredients in bread machine in order above. Use dough cycle and bake in oven.

OR

In large bowl dissolve yeast with 1 teaspoon of the sugar in 1/4 cup of the water until foamy to proof. Add remainder of the water, remainder of the sugar, and 1-1/4 cups flour to yeast mixture. Beat for 5 minutes with dough hooks on electric beater. Cover with a damp towel and let rise in an unheated oven for 1 hour. Add salt, oil, and remaining white bread flour. Mix until dough comes clean from bowl.

Turn onto floured board and knead for 10 minutes, sprinkling with flour as necessary to make a soft, malleable dough. Cover with dry towel and let rise for 1 hour. Punch down, cover with dry towel, and allow dough to rise for 30 minutes. Punch down again. Fashion into oval loaf. Place on greased baking sheet. Cover with dry towel and let rise for 30 minutes.

Brush dough with egg white. Bake for 45 minutes. Brush bread again and bake for 5 minutes longer or until browned on all sides.

ENTRÉES

ROASTED STUFFED CHICKEN (F)

Roasted and stuffed chicken is what my mother used to serve on Friday night. Here is how I prepare it:

Take an average size bird (fresh or frozen and thoroughly defrosted) and remove the gizzards,* which are usually wrapped in white paper and found in the large cavity. Then I wash the chicken thoroughly inside and out, removing all remaining gizzards from skeleton crevices. I really dig into the skeleton with my fingers to make sure nothing remains. Next, I sprinkle it with salt on the inside cavity. On the outer surface I season with salt, pepper, paprika, some garlic powder, poultry seasoning, or herbs such as parsley, sage, rosemary, and thyme (as in the song "Scarborough Fair").

Stuffing:

Although my mother's chicken was very good, I did not care for her stuffing. However, my mother-in-law's stuffing, I think, is great, see Mom Yellin's Bread Stuffing Kugel recipe on p. 108. You can either stuff the mixture inside large cavity of the chicken, or bake it as a kugel. Place the stuffed, or not, chicken in pan (the black roasting pans with the little white speckles are my favorites). I do not tie the bird nor do I baste it.

Cover the pan and bake at 350° for about 45 minutes to 1-1/2 hours, depending on size. Chicken will be ready when:

✿ you see no pink when you cut leg at the joint,
✿ you poke leg with a fork and juices that pour from pierce are clear,
✿ the leg wiggles easily,
✿ the little white button (on some poultry) pops out,
✿ meat thermometer reads 190° Fahrenheit

Some people cut up the gizzards, broil them, and use in stuffing mixture. I usually just place the washed liver and neck alongside the chicken in the pan to cook.

CHICKEN WITH ORANGES, APRICOTS, AND ALMONDS (F)

2 tablespoons canola oil
1 medium-sized white onion, finely chopped
3-1/2 pounds chicken, boned, and cubed
1 cup water
2 teaspoons ground cinnamon
1/2 teaspoon ground ginger
2 cups mandarin oranges
1 cup dried apricots, diced
1 tablespoon honey
1 cup slivered almonds, lightly toasted
1/3 teaspoon freshly ground black pepper
   pinch of salt

Makes 6 servings.

Heat oil over medium heat in a large heavy pot. Sauté onion until tender but not browned. Add chicken and brown on all sides.

Combine water, cinnamon, ginger, pepper, and salt and pour over chicken. Bring liquid to a boil. Cover the skillet tightly, lower the heat, and simmer chicken for 30 minutes, turning pieces occasionally.

Add oranges, apricots, and honey to pot, evenly distributing around the chicken, and cover with liquid. Cover pot again, and simmer for about 20 minutes, or until chicken is very tender. If the sauce becomes too dry and begins to stick to the bottom of the pot, stir in additional water as needed, 1/2 cup at a time.

Use slotted spoon to transfer chicken to a large serving platter. Stir about half the almonds into the sauce remaining in the pot; then spoon the sauce mixture over the chicken. Garnish the top with the remaining almonds.

CHICKEN IN RED WINE (F)

2 pounds chicken breast, boneless and skinless
1 tablespoon pareve margarine
1 tablespoon extra virgin olive oil
1 bunch green onions, sliced; reserve 1 tablespoon
1 cup kosher dry red wine
1/3 cup soy sauce
1/3 cup brown sugar
1/2 teaspoon ginger, minced
1/4 teaspoon garlic powder
4 teaspoons cornstarch
4 teaspoons water

Serves 4.

In a skillet, lightly brown chicken in margarine and oil, remove chicken from pan. Stir in green onions, wine, soy sauce, brown sugar, ginger, and garlic powder.

In a small dish, combine cornstarch with water, stir into wine mixture. Cook, stirring until sauce is clear and thickened.

Add chicken, turning to coat all sides with wine mixture. Cover and simmer 15 minutes, turning chicken once or twice during cooking. Serve over rice, bowties (farfel), or shell pasta; garnish with reserved green onions.

GEDEMPT
BRISKET POT ROAST (F)

    4 pounds beef brisket, well trimmed
OR
    4 pounds boneless chuck roast short ribs
    3 tablespoons canola oil
    2 large white onions, sliced
    2 scallions, sliced
    2 cloves garlic, minced
    2 large carrots, shredded
    2 stalks celery, diced
    1 pound button mushrooms, sliced
    2 teaspoons salt
  1/2 teaspoon paprika
    4 bay leaves
  1/2 teaspoon freshly ground black pepper
1-1/2 cups beef stock
  1/4 cup ketchup
    2 tablespoons brown sugar

Serves 6.

Heat the oil in a large, heavy pot and brown meat on all sides.

Add remaining ingredients, cover, and simmer stovetop for 1-1/2 to 2 hours, until meat is tender. Uncover pan and discard bay leaves.

Transfer meat to a cutting board. Remove vegetables from gravy and place in food processor. Purée vegetables and mix with gravy.

Thinly slice meat against the grain. Return meat to pan and pour puréed mixture over the meat. Stir to coat meat. Serve hot with kasha and bowties, boiled potatoes, noodles, or use for sandwiches.

CARROT TZIMMES WITH MEAT (F)

This dish, which is served frequently at Rosh Hashanah and Passover meals, is a sweetened stew that is sometimes served as a side dish when meat is not added. See Carrot Tzimmes p. 188.

```
 3  pounds beef brisket, well trimmed
1/2 box pitted prunes
 5  ounces dried apricots
 5  large carrots, cut in chunks
 2  40-ounce cans yams, drained
OR 10 orange yams, pared and cut into large chunks
 1  20-ounce can crushed pineapple, in own juice, not drained
1/2 cup brown sugar
 3  tablespoons lemon juice
1/2 teaspoon grated lemon rind
 4  packets kosher beef bouillon
1/2 cup honey
```

Preheat oven to 325°.   Serves 10.

Soak prunes and apricots in enough boiling water to cover. Drain and set aside liquid.

Brown meat on all sides. Place brisket in a large roasting pan and surround with carrots, yams, prunes, and apricots. Pour crushed pineapple with syrup over the vegetables and fruits. Sprinkle remaining bouillon packets over vegetables and fruit.

Sprinkle brown sugar, lemon rind, and lemon juice over all ingredients. Drizzle with honey. Cover pan and bake for 3 hours or until meat is tender. Add reserved liquid, as needed, to ingredients in pan. Season to taste with brown sugar or lemon juice.

PRAAKES, HOLISHKES, OR GALUPTZI
STUFFED CABBAGE (F)

The name of this dish depends on country origin of its cooks or their ancestors. In Jewish cuisine, it is very popular during the holiday of Sukkot.

1   2-pound head white or savoy cabbage, core removed
1   pound lean ground beef
1/4   cup white rice, cooked
1   large egg, beaten
1   medium yellow onion, grated
1   large carrot, grated
1/2   teaspoon salt
1/4   teaspoon freshly ground black pepper

Sauce:

4   tablespoons cooking oil
12   ounces tomato paste
5   tablespoons brown sugar
5   tablespoons white vinegar
1/2   cup golden or dark raisins (optional)

Preheat oven to 450°.   Makes 12-15 rolls.

Parboil whole head of cabbage for about 10 minutes. Separate leaves and be careful not to tear. Place leaves back into water and simmer for 5 minutes, until soft enough for wrapping filling. Trim away thick part at bottom of leaves and discard. In medium mixing bowl, combine all sauce ingredients.

In a large mixing bowl, combine beef, rice, egg, onion, carrot, salt, and pepper and mix thoroughly. Place a heaping tablespoon of filling in the center of each leaf and fold leaf to cover, tightly tucking ends in. Repeat until all filling is used. Chop remaining cabbage leaves and place on bottom of a 9" x 13" baking pan. With seam side down, place cabbage rolls over bed of chopped cabbage. Pour sauce over rolls to cover. Cover with foil and bake for 20 minutes. Reduce heat to 300° and bake for 2 more hours. Add water after 1 hour, if sauce becomes too thick.

CHOLENT (F)

2-1/2 pounds beef brisket, or top of round, well trimmed and
       cut into 6 large chunks
  1/3 cup canola oil
    3 cloves garlic, chopped fine
    2 medium yellow onions, diced
    3 quarts water
    1 cup lima beans, uncooked
  1/2 cup pearl barley
    2 large tomatoes, quartered
    2 stalks celery, quartered
  1/2 cup green bell pepper, chopped
    3 carrots, brushed and cut into large chunks
  1/2 teaspoon paprika
    1 tablespoon cilantro, chopped
    1 teaspoon salt
  1/2 teaspoon pepper
    2 bay leaves
    2 unbroken eggs, in the shell, washed

8 servings.

In a large, heavy pot with a tight fitting lid, sauté the garlic
and onion in oil. Add remaining ingredients, cover, and bring
to a boil.

Reduce heat to lowest setting. Place pot on a blech (sheet of
metal) and cook for 4-6 hours. Or place ingredients in a
baking pan and bake overnight at 200°. Check cholent
periodically to be sure there is enough water. Add 1/2 cup
water as needed.

Note: Kugel can be steamed in a round pan in the center of
cholent. The edges of kugel pan should be higher than cholent
ingredients. Pan will probably float on top.

ROASTED LAMB (F)

1 7-pound shoulder of lamb
3 tablespoons fresh lemon juice
1 tablespoon dried parsley flakes
1 teaspoon dried mint or basil, crushed
1/2 teaspoon dried rosemary, crushed
1/2 teaspoon onion salt
1/4 teaspoon pepper
2 cloves garlic, slivered
1/2 cup celery leaves, shredded
1/3 cup green bell pepper, cubed
mint jelly (optional)

Preheat oven to 325°.   6 servings.

Cut 1/2 inch wide pockets into lamb at 1 inch intervals. Brush meat and pockets with lemon juice. Combine parsley flakes, mint or basil, rosemary, onion salt, and pepper. Rub seasonings over meat and into pockets. Insert garlic slivers into meat pockets.

Place meat on a rack in a shallow roasting pan. Surround with celery leaves and bell pepper. Insert a meat thermometer. Roast for 1-3/4 hours for rare (140°), 2 hours for medium (160°), or 2-1/2 hours for well-done (170°). Let stand 15 minutes before carving. Serve with mint jelly and gravy.

LAMB GRAVY (F)

Remove lamb from roasting pan and keep warm. Allow fat in pan to congeal; skim and discard. Boil down natural gravy, leaving celery leaves, and green pepper in pan. Add 1 tablespoon of ketchup to enhance gravy flavor, if desired.

SALMON LOAF (M)

1 can red salmon, drained
1/4 cup yellow onion, chopped
1/4 cup carrot, grated
1/4 cup celery, chopped
1/4 cup green pepper, chopped
2 tablespoons sour cream
3/4 cup milk
2 slices white bread
3 large eggs, slightly beaten

Preheat oven to 350°.

Mix together first 6 ingredients. Soak bread in milk; add to salmon mixture. Add eggs and mix thoroughly. Pour into 2 quart baking dish. Bake for 45 minutes. Serve with sour cream.

FISH IN WINE (F)

1 pound flounder or orange roughy filets
1 large egg, beaten
1/3 cup flour, unbleached and presifted
1 cup chicken stock
2 ounces kosher dry white wine
3 tablespoons lemon juice

Coat fish with egg, then flour.

Place in heated pan and sauté in stock until golden brown on both sides.

Add wine and lemon juice. Continue to cook until liquid has almost entirely evaporated, about 5 minutes. Transfer to serving platter and garnish with lemon slices.

MESQUITE SMOKED SALMON (P)

1 1-pound salmon filet, 1-1/2 inch thick
5 sprigs fresh thyme
3 sprigs fresh parsley
5 stems green onions
1 large sprig basil
1 small yellow onion chopped
  salt and pepper to taste

3 servings.

Soak 1 cup of mesquite wood chips in water. Heat regular barbeque briquettes to medium temperature. Place 1/2 cup of the soaked chips on top of briquettes.

Oil cooking rack of grill and place green onion and basil sprig on it. Sprinkle salmon filet with salt and pepper and lay it skin side down, on top of green onion and basil.

Place chopped onion, parsley and thyme sprigs on salmon. Close lid of grill and cook for 10 minutes. Add remaining 1/2 cup of wood chips cook for additional 10 minutes.

COLD BAKED SALMON WITH CUCUMBER SAUCE (P)

    1 2-pound salmon filet
  2-3 tablespoons pareve margarine
    1 leek, thinly sliced
  1/2 cup dry white wine
  1/2 teaspoon dried thyme
       salt and freshly ground pepper to taste

Preheat oven to 425°.   8 servings.

Remove skin from fish. Cut a piece of parchment paper to size of baking dish and grease with margarine; set aside. Spray a baking dish with non-stick baking spray or margarine. Distribute leek rings on bottom of pan. Arrange fish in pan in one layer.

Pour wine over fish. Sprinkle with thyme, salt and pepper. Set parchment paper over fish. Bake for 12 to 15 minutes until fish is opaque inside. Place fish on a platter and cool to room temperature. Serve with Cucumber Sauce.

CUCUMBER SAUCE (M)

    1 medium cucumber, pared
  1/2 cup sour cream
  1/4 cup mayonnaise
    1 tablespoon fresh parsley, chopped
    2 teaspoons yellow onion, grated
    2 teaspoons white vinegar
  1/4 teaspoon salt
       dash pepper

Cut cucumber in half lengthwise and scoop out seeds. Blend in food processor with remaining ingredients until smooth. Chill.

185

LOX WINGS AND POTATOES (P)

At a kosher delicatessen, purchase as many lox wings as you want. Peel some potatoes, how many is your choice; cut potatoes into large chunks. Put lox wings and potatoes into a pot and cover with water.

Cover with a lid and boil until the potatoes are soft; drain water. Serve with butter or sour cream and chopped parsley or chives for the potatoes, if desired.

LAYERED FISH AND POTATO CASSEROLE (M)

```
  5   medium white potatoes, thinly sliced
  2   cups cod, cooked
  1   cup tuna, canned or fresh cooked
  2   tablespoons butter
  2   large white onions, sliced
1/2   teaspoon freshly ground black pepper
1-1/2 teaspoons salt*
  2   large eggs, beaten
1-1/2 cups light cream*
```

Preheat oven to 350°.   4 servings.

In heavy skillet, brown onions in melted butter. Sprinkle potatoes with salt and pepper and toss.

Arrange alternate layers of potatoes, fish, and onions in buttered 8" x 8" baking pan, starting and ending with potatoes.

Combine eggs and cream and beat; pour over the contents of baking dish. Bake 45 minutes until lightly browned. Do not freeze.

CHEESE BLINTZES (M)

1   cup flour, unbleached and presifted
2   large eggs, beaten
1-1/2   cups milk
1   tablespoon canola oil

Combine flour, eggs, milk, and oil and beat until smooth. Drop 1/4 cup of batter into the center of a heated 6-inch nonstick skillet or inverted crepe pan. Gently move pan so batter spreads evenly, and cook until golden (about 45 seconds). Loosen edges, if necessary, and turn out onto a kitchen towel with cooked side up. Repeat until all the batter is used.

Filling:

1   pound farmer cheese or cottage cheese, drained
1/4   cup sugar (add more to taste)
1   large egg, beaten
    dash cinnamon

Makes 18.

Mix together all filling ingredients. Spread cooked side of crepe with about 2 tablespoons of filling in a log shape. Fold two ends of crepe over filling and then fold over long sides to form log shape.

Place blintzes, with seam side down, into a well-buttered pan. Cook until golden brown. Serve with sour cream and/or preserves.

Variation:

Fill crepes with prepared apple, cherry or blueberry filling.

VEGETABLES, SIDE DISHES, AND SALADS

STEAMED WHOLE GREEN BEANS AND MUSHROOMS (P)

       1 pound whole green beans, frozen or fresh
    1/2 pound fresh button mushrooms, sliced
       1 small yellow onion, chopped
       1 tablespoon canola or extra virgin olive oil
         lemon juice, to taste

If fresh green beans are used, wash them and cut off the ends. Sauté mushrooms and onion in oil until tender.

Place green beans into a saucepan with 1/2 cup water. Steam for about 4 minutes, or until slightly tender but still crispy. Do not overcook.

Add sautéed mushrooms and onions. Sprinkle with lemon juice.

CARROT TZIMMES (P)

        3 cups sliced carrots, parboiled
    1-1/2 cups sliced yams
        9 large pitted prunes
      1/2 cup crushed pineapple in own juice, not drained
      1/3 cup honey or brown sugar
      1/3 cup orange juice concentrate
      1/2 teaspoon cinnamon
      1/4 teaspoon salt

Preheat oven to 250°.   6 servings.

Mix all ingredients together in a large bowl and pour into a well-greased 2 quart casserole. Cover and bake 3 hours.

GLAZED CARROTS (P)

1   pound baby carrots
4   tablespoons brown sugar
4   tablespoons canola oil
1/2   cup honey
1   tablespoon lemon peel
      dash ginger
      salted water to cover

6 servings.

Cut carrots into slices and cover with salted water. Boil for 10 minutes. Reduce heat and add honey, sugar, and oil. Simmer until liquid is absorbed and carrots are glazed (about 30 minutes). Sprinkle with lemon peel and ginger.

MOCK KISHKA (P)

This is a variation of the popular stuffed derma (or stuffed goose or chicken neck) that is often served as a side dish at celebration dinners.

1   8-ounce box Tam Tam crackers
1   large yellow onion, grated
2   large carrots, grated
3   stalks celery, finely chopped
2   ounces pareve margarine
1/2   teaspoon salt
1/4   teaspoon pepper
1   teaspoon paprika

Preheat oven to 425°.   16 servings.

Place all ingredients in the bowl of a food processor that has been fitted with the steel blade. Process to a smooth consistency. Divide mixture in half; place each half on a piece of aluminum foil and form into a long roll 2 inches in diameter.

Tightly seal edges of foil around roll and bake for 30 minutes. Unwrap and cut into 1-inch slices. Serve as an appetizer or side dish.

189

KASHA VARNISHKES
KASHA AND BOWTIES (P)

4 cups kasha (buckwheat groats)
2 large eggs, beaten
6 tablespoons canola oil
8 cups boiling water
4 medium yellow onions
8 ounces bowtie (farfel) noodles
   salt and pepper, to taste

Serves 8.

Place 3 tablespoons of the oil in large frying pan and sauté onions until golden; pour into bowl and set aside.

Place remaining 3 tablespoons oil in pan. Add kasha and brown until crispy and all grains are separated.

Stir in eggs and water. Cover pan and bring mixture to a boil. Season with salt and pepper. Lower heat and simmer for about 20 minutes or until tender, stirring occasionally.

Add onions to kasha mixture.

Cook bowties according to package directions and drain. After draining, mix with the kasha. Serve with Gedempt and top with gravy.

MEAL APPEAL

A meal should look as attractive on a plate as it is tasty and well balanced. Make a brown and white meal colorful by adding garnishes such as fresh fruit slices, grapes, or red bell pepper strips. Accompany it with fresh steamed asparagus, broccoli, or whole green beans.

CUCUMBER SALAD (P)

2 cucumbers, peeled and thinly sliced
1 medium yellow onion, thinly sliced

Combine ingredients. Use with salad dressing mixture below.

TOMATO AND BELL PEPPER SALAD (P)

2 tomatoes, cut into wedges and then halves
2 scallions, chopped
1 each green, red, and yellow bell peppers, diced

Combine ingredients. Use with salad dressing mixture below.

CUCUMBER, TOMATO AND BELL PEPPER SALAD P)

Combine all ingredients in above two mixtures. Use with salad dressing mixture below.

VINAIGRETTE SALAD DRESSING (P)

1/4 cup sugar or sugar substitute equivalent
1/4 cup vinegar
1/2 cup water
1/8 cup canola oil
1/4 teaspoon each garlic powder and oregano
     salt and freshly ground black pepper, to taste

Mix sugar, vinegar, water, and oil in a container with a lid. Shake until thoroughly mixed. Add garlic, oregano, salt, and pepper and shake again, then pour over vegetables. Marinate in refrigerator overnight.

EGGPLANT SALAD (P)

2 tablespoons extra virgin olive oil
1 small yellow onion, finely chopped
2 cloves garlic, minced
1/2 large red bell pepper
1 cup fresh button mushrooms, chopped
1 medium unpeeled eggplant, chopped
1/4 cup black olives, pitted and chopped
1-1/4 tablespoons red wine vinegar
1/3 cup dry wine
1/2 teaspoon brown sugar
1/4 teaspoon oregano
1/2 teaspoon salt
1/4 teaspoon freshly ground black pepper
2 tablespoons pine nuts

Makes 3 cups.

Sauté onion, garlic, and green pepper in oil until tender. Add mushrooms and eggplant. Cover pan and simmer, stirring often, until eggplant is very soft.

Add remaining ingredients; continue to cook for about 20 more minutes until everything is well blended. Allow mixture to cool and serve with pita or thinly sliced party bread.

EGGPLANT MEDLEY

Ingredients for Eggplant Salad, above
2 tablespoons brown sugar
1 large ripe tomato
2 tablespoons lime juice
2 cups shredded carrots
6 scallions, chopped
2 tablespoons fresh basil, chopped

Makes 4 cups.

Combine all ingredients. Cook for about 20 minutes until everything is well blended. Serve warm as side dish with meat, poultry or fish.

LATKES (Pancakes)

VEGETABLE LATKES (P)

2 cups fresh button mushrooms, shredded
2 cups carrots, shredded
2 cups zucchini, shredded
2 tablespoons garlic, chopped
2 large eggs, beaten
1/2 cup flour, unbleached and presifted
    salt and pepper, to taste

4 servings.

Combine mushrooms, carrots and zucchini with garlic, salt, and pepper. Add egg, stir, and then add flour. Stir everything until thoroughly mixed.

Heat about 1/4 inch of oil in large frying pan. When bubbles form after small drops of water are added to oil, it is ready.

Drop batter into hot oil by the tablespoonful and flatten with spoon. Fry mixture on both sides until golden. Add more oil if necessary and repeat until all of the batter is used. Remove from pan and drain on paper towels.

Latkes are best served warm, right after cooking. Reheated latkes lose their crispness.

LATKES AND HANUKKAH

Since the Middle Ages, Sephardic Jews have traditionally eaten cheese latkes. It is said that this custom evolved from the biblical story of Judith. An Assyrian general named Holofernes was sent to destroy Palestine. Judith, a Jewish widow, told him he would be victorious and she was invited into his tent. She stuffed him with cheese so he would become thirsty. He drank wine to quench his thirst and when he was asleep in a drunken stupor, she...

...I can't go on. What happened is too horrible to tell. However, a victory over the now leaderless Assyrian forces followed.

The story of Judith, which brings to light the forces of good and evil, was thought to have been an inspiration to the Maccabees. To commemorate the event, people started baking cheese-filled things for Hanukkah. However, the largest proportion of American Jews are Ashkenazic and it is their tradition that has become the most popular in this country. Potato latkes (pancakes) made with grated potatoes, eggs, and onions, and fried in goose fat became a popular item and a traditional Hanukkah food.

CHEESE LATKES (M)

2 cups farmer cheese or large curd cottage cheese, drained
1 cup sifted flour, unbleached and presifted
1/2 teaspoon salt
2 large eggs, separated
2 tablespoons sugar

6 servings.

Beat egg yolks with sugar and salt. Add cottage cheese and flour. Beat egg whites until stiff and fold into mixture.

Pour 1/2 inch of oil into a large frying pan or griddle. Drop batter into hot oil by the tablespoonful and flatten with spoon. Fry mixture on both sides until crisp. Add more oil if necessary and repeat until all of the batter is used. Serve plain or sprinkled with sugar and cinnamon or preserves.

Uncle Sam Yellin from Stratford-Laurel Springs, N. J. made the best potato latkes. He used to serve them with leg of lamb smothered in thick brown gravy. My husband, Steve, picked up where Uncle Sam left off with the potato latkes. He is very particular about how his potatoes are grated. They must be done by hand on the medium holes of the grater. He also must use his favorite large wooden spoon when placing the batter into the hot oil.

STEVE'S POTATO LATKES (P)

6 medium white potatoes, grated and drained
2 large eggs, beaten
1 teaspoon salt
1/4 teaspoon freshly ground black pepper
1 large yellow onion
1 heaping tablespoon flour, unbleached and presifted
    enough canola oil for frying

6 servings.

Grate potatoes.* Drain excess liquid. Stir in the rest of the ingredients. Heat about 1/2 inch of oil in large frying pan. When bubbles form after small drops of water are added to oil, it is ready. Drop batter into hot oil with a large spoon and flatten. Fry mixture on both sides until crisp. Add more oil, if necessary, and repeat until all of the batter is used.

Remove from pan and place on paper towels. Latkes are best served warm, right after cooking. Reheated latkes lose their crispness. Serve with applesauce. For a dairy dish, serve with sour cream or smoked salmon sauce.

SMOKED SALMON SAUCE (M)

8 ounces soft cream cheese with salmon
1/2 cup sour cream
1/4 cup mayonnaise
1/2 teaspoon chopped fresh dill

In a small bowl, stir together ingredients until well blended.

STUFFED POTATO LATKES (F)

A friend from Byelorus, or Byelorussia told me potato latkes originated there and she prepared a wonderful luncheon meal for me with latkes stuffed with ground meat. She said that as of about 10 years ago, when she left her country, Jewish people where she lived did not practice kashruth. The ground beef is usually mixed with ground pork, but for me, and for the sake of this book, my friend mixed it with ground turkey. Latkes prepared in this manner are frequently topped with sour cream.

1/4 pound mixed ground beef and ground turkey
1   small yellow onion
1/2 teaspoon each dried dill, parsley, and caraway seeds
1   large egg, beaten
    pinch of salt and pepper

Prepare Steve's Potato Latke recipe (p. 195), but use:

3   tablespoons of flour

6 servings.

Thoroughly combine everything except latke batter.

Heat about 1/2 inch of oil in large frying pan. When bubbles form after small drops of water are added to oil, it is ready.

Drop batter into hot oil with a large spoon and flatten. Cover with ground beef and top with more batter. Repeat until there are several patties in pan. Cover pan with a lid. Fry mixture on both sides until crisp. Add more oil if necessary and repeat until all of the batter is used.

Remove from pan and drain on paper towels. Latkes are best served warm, right after cooking. Reheated latkes lose their crispness. Serve with applesauce. For a dairy dish, serve with sour cream.

WHITE AND SWEET POTATO LATKES (P)

2 cups sweet potatoes, finely grated
2 cups white potatoes, finely grated
2 medium yellow onion, finely grated
1/2 cup matzo meal
4 large eggs, beaten
1-1/2 teaspoons salt
   pinch of pepper
   enough canola oil for frying

6 servings.

Combine everything and stir thoroughly. Heat about 1/2 inch of oil in large frying pan. When bubbles form after small drops of water are added to oil, it is ready.

Drop batter into hot oil by the tablespoonful and flatten with spoon. Fry mixture on both sides until crisp. Add more oil if necessary and repeat until all of the batter is used.

Remove from pan and drain on paper towels. Latkes are best served warm, right after cooking. Reheated latkes lose their crispness.

NO-FRY POTATO LATKES (P)

3 cups all-purpose potatoes, boiled and mashed
2 tablespoons pareve margarine
1 large egg, beaten
   salt and pepper, to taste

Preheat oven to 350°.

4 servings.

Mix potatoes, margarine, egg, salt and pepper together and form into patties. Place on greased baking sheet and bake 30 to 45 minutes or until browned.

THE LATKE SONG

By Debbie Friedman

Samba tempo — Cm

I am so mixed up that I can - not tell you,___ I'm
Ev - ery ho - li - day has foods so spe - cial,___ I'd
It's im - por - tant that I have an un - der - stand - ing___ of

sit - ting in this blen - der tur - ning brown. I've
like to have that same at - ten - tion too. I
what it is that I'm sup - posed to do. You

made friends with the on - ions and the flo - ur,___ and the
do not want to spend life in this blen - der,___
see,___ there are ma - ny who are home - less,___ with no

cook is scout - ing o - il___ in town. I
won - der - ing what I'm sup - posed to do.
jobs, no clothes and ve - ry lit - tle food. It's

sit here won - dering what will 'come of me,___ I
Mat - za and char - o - set are for Pe - sach,___ chopped
so im - por - tant that we all re - mem - ber,___ that

198

can't be ea - ten look - ing as I do. I
li - ver____ and chal - lah for Shab - bat.
while we have most of the things we need, we

need some - one to take me out and cook me,____ or I'll
Blin - tzes on Sha - vu - ot are de - li - cious,____ and ge -
must re - mem - ber those who have so lit - tle,____ we must

really end up in a roy - al stew. I am a lat - ke,____ I'm a
fil - te fish no ho - li - day's with - out.
help them, we must be the ones to feed.

CHORUS

lat - ke,____ and I am wait - ing____ for____ Cha - nu - kah to come. I am a

lat - ke,____ I'm a lat - ke,____ and I am wait - ing for Cha - nu - kah to

come.

3. It's im-

come. I am a lat - ke,____ I'm a lat - ke,____ and I am

wait - ing____ for____ Cha - nu - kah to come. I am a lat - ke,____ I'm a

lat - ke,____ and I am wait - ing for Cha - nu - kah to

come.

199

CORN LATKES (P or M)

2 cups cooked corn (off the cob or canned kernels)
2 large eggs, beaten
1/2 teaspoon salt
1/2 cup flour, unbleached and presifted
1/2 cup water or milk

6 servings.

Combine eggs, add salt, flour, and liquid to make a smooth batter. Add corn and stir thoroughly. Heat about 1/2 inch of oil in large frying pan. When bubbles form after small drops of water are added to oil, it is ready.

Drop batter into hot oil by the tablespoonful and flatten with spoon. Fry mixture on both sides until golden. Add more oil if necessary and repeat until all of the batter is used. Remove from pan and drain on paper towels. Latkes are best served warm, right after cooking. Reheated latkes lose their crispness.

FRUIT LATKES (P)

2 cups flour, unbleached and presifted
1/2 teaspoon salt
3 teaspoons baking powder
1/2 teaspoon ground cinnamon
2 large eggs, beaten
1-1/3 cups orange juice
1 6-ounce can crushed pineapple, in own juice drained
powdered sugar for sprinkling

4 servings.

Sift together flour, salt, and baking powder, and cinnamon.
Beat in eggs and orange juice. Add crushed pineapple. Heat about 1/8 inch of oil in large frying pan. When bubbles form after small drops of water are added to oil, it is ready.

Drop batter into hot oil by the tablespoonful and flatten with spoon. Fry mixture on both sides until golden. Add more oil if necessary and repeat until all of the batter is used. Sprinkle with powdered sugar. Latkes are best served warm, right after cooking. Reheated latkes lose their crispness.

MATZO MEAL LATKES (P)

1/2 cup matzo meal
1 tablespoon sugar
3/4 cup cold water
3 large eggs, separated
 oil for frying

Makes 10.

Combine matzo meal and sugar.

Beat egg yolks slightly and combine with water. Add egg mixture to dry ingredients. Allow to stand 1/2 hour. Beat egg whites until stiff and fold into matzo meal mixture. Heat about 1/4 inch of oil in large frying pan. When bubbles form after small drops of water are added to oil, it is ready.

Drop batter into hot oil by the tablespoonful and flatten with spoon. Fry mixture on both sides until golden. Add more oil if necessary and repeat until all of the batter is used. Serve with granulated sugar. Latkes are best served warm, right after cooking. Reheated latkes lose their crispness.

MATZO BREI (P)

2 matzot
1 cup water
2 large eggs, beaten
1/2 teaspoon salt
1 tablespoon canola oil

2 servings.

Break matzot into small pieces and soak in a deep bowl with water for 2-3 minutes. Drain and squeeze out water. In a medium bowl beat the eggs with salt and add softened matzo. Mix well.

Heat about 1/4 inch of oil in no-stick frying pan. Fry mixture on both sides until crisp. Sprinkle with cinnamon and sugar or top with jelly, applesauce, or sour cream.

201

LATKE HINTS

1. Latkes are best served warm, right after cooking. Reheated latkes lose their crispness.

2. Line a baking sheet with foil and lay cooked latkes in a single layer on foil. Place uncovered pan in freezer for 10 minutes to flash freeze. Transfer latkes to freezer bags and freeze until ready to use. Warm frozen latkes in oven set at 400° for about 15 minutes or until hot.

3. The best latkes are about 4" in diameter. When they are too large they tend to cook unevenly; if too small, they may become too crisp.

4. For a finer grated consistency — If you use a food processor to grate potatoes and only have one size hole for grating, return coarse shreds to processor. Use steel blade as you pulse process to desired consistency.

5. If you want to have the taste of fried latkes, but do not want the fat, pour the batter into individual muffin tins sprayed with a non-stick baking spray and bake 1/2 hour at 350° until firm. Especially good for potato latkes.

6. Drain liquid from potato mixture before frying potato latkes.

7. Prepare latkes and blot with paper towels.

8. Serve with sour cream, applesauce, or granulated or powdered sugar.

DESSERTS

HONEY CAKE (P)

4 large eggs, beaten
1/3 cup canola oil
1-1/4 cups brown sugar
1 cup honey
1 cup coffee, decaffeinated or regular
1 6-ounce can frozen, undiluted orange juice, thawed
2-1/2 cups flour, unbleached and presifted
1 cup whole wheat flour
1-1/2 teaspoons baking powder
2 teaspoons baking soda
1 teaspoon ground cinnamon
1 teaspoon ground allspice
1/8 teaspoon salt
1/2 cup chopped walnuts
1/2 cup white raisins

Preheat oven to 300°.   Makes 2 loaf cakes.

Thoroughly combine eggs, oil, sugar, and honey. Add coffee and orange juice. Sift together dry ingredients and gradually add to egg mixture. Beat until very smooth. Add walnuts and raisins and stir.

Grease and flour two loaf pans and pour in mixture. Bake 1 hour and 10 minutes or until springy to the touch. Remove from pan and cool.

This cake tastes best when flavor has had a chance to develop, so wrap and serve the next day.

HAMANTASHEN (P)

This filled cookie is enjoyed during the celebration of Purim (p. 227). It is formed into a triangle, the shape of Haman's hat.

4 cups flour, unbleached and presifted
4 teaspoons baking powder
1 teaspoon salt
1 cup sugar
1/2 pound pareve margarine
4 large eggs, beaten
1 teaspoon vanilla extract
1 teaspoon lemon extract

Preheat oven to 350°.

Combine flour, baking powder, salt, and sugar. With a pastry cutter, cut in margarine. Set aside.

Beat together eggs, vanilla and lemon extract; add to flour mixture and blend well. Cover and chill for 2 hours (or dough can be refrigerated for several days).

Divide dough into 4 balls.

On a floured surface, roll out a ball of dough to 1/8 inch thickness with a floured rolling pin. With a 3-inch round cookie cutter or inverted glass, cut cookie dough.

Filling:

Fill with lekvar (prune jam), prepared pie cherries, lemon pie filling, or prepared poppy seed filling. Add chopped walnuts and a small amount of lemon juice to prune and poppy seed fillings if desired.

Place 1 heaping teaspoonful of filling on each circle. Fold 3 sides of dough up over filling to fashion a triangular-shaped cookie. Pinch dough together.

Place on well-greased baking sheet and bake for 15 to 20 minutes, until light brown.

HANUKKAH COOKIES (P)

1/2 cup vegetable shortening
1/4 cup pareve margarine
1 cup sugar
2 large eggs, beaten
1 teaspoon vanilla extract
2-1/2 cups flour, unbleached and presifted
1 teaspoon baking powder
1 teaspoon salt

Preheat oven to 400°.   Makes about 4 dozen.

Blend shortening, margarine, sugar, eggs, and vanilla thoroughly. Combine flour, baking powder, and salt; add to sugar mixture. Chill for 1 hour.

On lightly floured surface, roll dough to 1/8 inch thickness with floured rolling-pin. Cut with Hanukkah cookie cutters and place on ungreased baking sheet.

Sprinkle with colored or granulated sugar or jimmies; bake for 6 to 8 minutes or until slightly browned around edges.

BUBBIE'S STRUDEL (P)

My Bubbie used to make the best strudel. It was not like the apple strudel that is usually sold in the delis or bakeries. Hers was embellished with nuts, coconut, jam, and raisins. I haven't tasted any bakery strudel like hers.

Dough:

2-1/2 cups flour, unbleached and presifted
2 tablespoons sugar
1/2 teaspoon salt
1 teaspoon baking powder
4 tablespoons canola oil
8 tablespoons warm water
2 large eggs, beaten

Continued on next page.

205

Sift dry ingredients together. Add oil and eggs, and water to bind.

Turn out onto a floured board. Knead until smooth and spongy. Set in bowl, sprinkle with flour, cover with plastic wrap, and chill 30 minutes.

Divide dough into five balls. With a floured roller, roll each ball to 1/8 inch thickness. Cut into long 3 inch wide strips. Brush dough with oil.

Filling:

1 15-ounce box white raisins
1 pound nuts, chopped
2 teaspoons ground cinnamon
1 cup sweetened shredded coconut
1 10-ounce jar orange marmalade
   oil for brushing

Preheat oven to 400°.   Makes about 40 pieces.

Rinse raisins in colander under hot water. Mix together with the rest of the filling ingredients. Divide into five portions.

Spread one portion over a brushed and rolled-out piece of dough. Bring edges up and pinch together at the top to form a long log. Repeat until all dough is used.

Place logs on well-oiled baking pan. Turn to coat. Every 1-1/2 inches, cut the logs to about 3/4 of the way through. Bake 40 to 50 minutes until browned. Remove from oven. Cut logs to separate. Cool on a cake rack and serve.

GIANT APPLE STRUDEL (P)

<u>Dough</u>:

1-1/4 cups flour, unbleached and presifted
1/2 teaspoon baking powder
1/4 teaspoon salt
1 tablespoon sugar
4 tablespoons warm water
2 tablespoons canola oil
1 large egg, beaten

Sift dry ingredients together.

Add oil, egg, and water to bind. Turn out onto a floured board.
Knead until smooth and spongy.

Set in bowl, sprinkle with flour, cover with plastic wrap, and
chill 30 minutes.

<u>Filling</u>:

3 pounds tart apples, pared and sliced
1 teaspoon ground cinnamon
1/4 cup sugar
1/2 cup raisins
1 teaspoon vanilla extract
1 teaspoon lemon juice
1/4 teaspoon allspice

Preheat oven to 350°.   20 servings.

Combine ingredients and mix thoroughly. Roll dough very
thin, to length of standard baking sheet.

Place dough on greased baking sheet (sides will be hanging
over edge). Brush with oil.

Spread apple mixture along long end. Fold remaining dough
over apples and pinch edges together.

Brush top with beaten egg. Bake 50 minutes until browned.
Lift off pan with <u>three</u> spatulas (you will need another hand).

JEWISH APPLE CAKE (P)

4 medium tart apples, pared, and thinly sliced
5 teaspoons sugar
2 teaspoons ground cinnamon
3 cups flour, unbleached and presifted
3 teaspoons baking powder
2 cups sugar
1 cup canola oil
4 large eggs, beaten
1/4 cup orange juice
2-1/2 teaspoons vanilla extract
    pinch of salt

Preheat oven to 350°.   12 servings.

Mix apples with cinnamon and sugar; set aside. Sift flour and baking powder together. Add remaining ingredients and beat together. Pour 1/3 of the batter into a greased tube pan; add 1/2 of the apples. Repeat layers, finishing with batter. Bake 1-1/2 hours or until cake tests done. Cool 20 minutes before removing from pan.

BANANA CAKE (P)

1/2 pound pareve margarine
2-1/4 cups sugar
3 large eggs, separated
1-1/2 teaspoons vanilla extract
1-1/2 cups mashed ripe bananas
3 cups flour, unbleached and presifted
1-1/2 teaspoons baking powder
1-1/2 teaspoons baking soda
3/4 cup hot water
1 cup chopped walnuts

Preheat oven to 350°.

Continued on next page.

208

Banana Cake continued.

Cream margarine and sugar in a large mixing bowl. Add egg yolks, vanilla, and bananas. Combine flour and baking powder. Add baking soda to hot water.

Add wet and dry ingredients alternately to batter. Fold in nuts. Beat egg whites stiff and fold into batter. Pour into large ungreased tube pan and bake for 1-1/4 hours or until cake tests done. Cool 20 minutes before removing from pan.

RUGALA (M)

RUGALA DOUGH

8 ounces cream cheese, softened
2 sticks margarine, softened
2 cups flour, unbleached and presifted

Preheat oven to 350°.   Makes 48 pieces.

In mixing bowl or food processor, cream the margarine and cream cheese. Beat in the flour, a little at a time. Knead the dough lightly until all the flour is mixed in. If the dough is sticky, dust it with flour, 1 tablespoon at a time, and knead.

Divide dough into four balls and cover with plastic wrap. Refrigerate 2 hours or up to 2 days. Roll each portion into a 9-inch circle on a board dusted lightly with flour or powdered sugar until about 1/8 inch thick. With a pastry wheel or knife, cut circle into 12 pie-shaped wedges. Spread with one of the fillings below.

Continued on next page.

RUGALA FILLING

RAISIN AND NUT FILLING (P)

1 cup sugar
2 tablespoons ground cinnamon
1 cup finely chopped walnuts or pecans
1/2 cup raisins (optional)

Combine sugar and cinnamon. Sprinkle over prepared rolled out and cut dough; sprinkle with nuts and raisins. Press ingredients down into dough with rolling pin. *Follow instructions below.

JAM FILLING (P)

Combine 1 cup ground almonds and 1 cup strawberry, apricot, or raspberry jam or preserves, or use 2 cups of jam or preserves without nuts. Divide into four portions and spread on rolled out and cut dough. * Follow instructions below.

CHOCOLATE CHIP FILLING (P)

Divide 2 cups miniature semisweet chocolate chips into four portions and spread on rolled out and cut dough.

*Separate the dough (cut through again if necessary). Beginning at the wide edge, roll dough up toward the point, folding into a crescent shape. Pinch in the ends to seal.

Place on ungreased baking sheets about 1 inch apart with point of triangle down. Sprinkle with sugar if powdered sugar was not used when rolling out the dough. Repeat until all dough and filling is used.

Refrigerate 20 minutes before baking. Bake 20 to 25 minutes or until golden, brushing with melted butter after 15 minutes if desired.

STICKY BUNS (M)

<u>Dough</u>:

    1 tablespoon warm water, 120° to 130° Fahrenheit
1-1/2 teaspoons active dry yeast
  1/4 cup milk, scalded
  1/2 cup butter
    1 large egg, beaten
  1/2 cup sour cream
  1/2 teaspoon vanilla extract
1/4 cup white sugar
  3/4 teaspoons salt
    3 cups flour

Makes 24.

Dissolve yeast in water to proof and let sit until foamy.

Add butter to scalded milk and stir to melt. Add egg, sour cream, vanilla, sugar, and salt and mix thoroughly.

Add yeast mixture and flour. Knead to mix thoroughly. If dough is too sticky, add more flour, 1 tablespoon at a time. Place mixture in a greased bowl and cover. Refrigerate overnight. Will keep for about 3 days in refrigerator.

Punch down dough and divide in half. Roll 1/2 the prepared dough, on a floured board with floured rolling-pin. Fashion into a long, narrow rectangle 4 inches wide and 1/4 inch thick. Prepare baking pan.

<u>For pan</u>:

1/3 cup butter, melted, reserving 4 tablespoons
1/2 cup dark brown sugar
1/4 cup dark Karo syrup
1/3 cup chopped walnuts or pecans

Place reserved 4 tablespoons of butter, brown sugar, and Karo syrup on bottom of 9"x 13" pan and stir to combine. Sprinkle with nuts, and set aside.

Continued on next page.

Sticky Buns continued.

<u>Filling</u>:

  2 tablespoons dark Karo syrup, divided
1/2 cup dark brown sugar, divided
  2 tablespoons cinnamon, divided
1/2 cup chopped walnuts divided
1/2 cup chopped raisins (optional), divided

Preheat oven to 375°.

Brush dough with 1/2 of remaining melted butter. Drizzle with 1 tablespoon Karo syrup and sprinkle with 1/4 cup of the brown sugar, 1 tablespoon cinnamon, 1/4 cup chopped walnuts, and 1/4 cup optional raisins.

From the long edge, roll dough jellyroll fashion. Repeat with remaining dough, butter, and filling. Cut into 1-inch slices.

Lay slices in prepared pan, with pinwheel spiral face-up. Cover sticky buns with towel. Let rise until doubled, about 30-40 minutes.

Bake for 20-25 minutes. Place pan on cooling rack for 1 minute to let syrup settle, then invert onto wax paper and cool. Can be frozen.

SCHNECKEN (M)

Use Sticky Bun Dough recipe. Do not follow instructions "for pan." Spread each portion of rolled out dough with one of the fillings in Rugala recipe on p. 209.

From the long edge, roll dough jellyroll fashion. Repeat with remaining dough, butter, and filling. Cut into 1-1/2-inch logs.

Lay logs in buttered 9"x 13" pan, just barely touching, with seam-side down. Cover schnecken with towel. Let rise until doubled, about 30-40 minutes. Sprinkle with granulated sugar. Bake for 20-25 minutes. Can be frozen.

TAYGLACH (P)

6 large eggs, beaten
1/4 cup canola oil
3-1/2 cups flour, unbleached and presifted
1-1/2 teaspoons baking powder
1-1/2 teaspoons ground ginger
1 cup chopped almonds, walnuts, or pecans
1-1/4 cups honey
    dash salt
    poppy seeds

Preheat oven to 450°.   Makes 3 dozen.

Combine eggs, salt, oil, flour, and baking powder. Place dough on floured board and knead until smooth. Add up to 1/2 cup additional flour (1 tablespoon at a time) as needed, if dough seems to be too sticky.

Divide dough into small portions, about 1/2 cup each. On lightly floured surface, roll each portion with both hands into a 10- to 12-inch rope. Cut each rope into 12 pieces. Place on ungreased baking sheet, making sure sides do not touch.

Bake 10 to 15 minutes until golden brown on bottom. Cool.

Heat honey to boiling in large saucepan. Add ginger. Reduce heat and cook for about 5 minutes, or until syrup reaches 260° on a candy thermometer. Carefully add baked pieces. Cook for about 10 minutes, stirring occasionally with a wooden spoon. Add nuts and mix thoroughly to distribute evenly onto tayglach.

Continue cooking until cookies are golden brown. Spoon onto large baking sheet lined with foil. Flatten cookies to about 1/2 inch thick, using a wet rolling pin or wooden spoon. Turn tayglach over onto a board and peel off foil. Sprinkle with poppy seeds.

When the tayglach have hardened, cut into 1-1/2 inch diamond-shaped pieces.

AUNT MYRNA'S MANDELBROIT (P)

The translation of mandelbroit is "almond bread." It is also known as "kmishbroit." I do not know what kmish means but do know it has absolutely nothing to do with "knish." This medium-hard cookie is the Jewish version of the Italian Biscotti. Aunt Myrna always kept a metal tin can filled with it. We used to sit around her kitchen table talking and laughing as we eat these cookies with a cup of hot tea. They are great for dunking.

3	large eggs, beaten
1	cup canola oil
1	teaspoon vanilla extract
1	cup sugar
1-1/2	teaspoons baking powder
3	cups flour, unbleached and presifted
1	cup slivered almonds or chocolate chips

Preheat oven to 350°.   Makes about 36 cookies.

Beat together eggs, vanilla, and oil. Combine sugar, flour, and baking powder and add to egg mixture. Add nuts or chocolate chips.

Knead dough to mix everything together thoroughly. Dough may be oily.

Divide into two balls. On ungreased baking sheet, form long loaves 2 inches wide and about 1 inch high.

Bake for 30 minutes. Remove from oven and slice into 1-inch bars. Lay cookies on their sides and bake for 10 more minutes to brown.

214

AUNT SYLVIA'S SPRITZ COOKIES

Aunt Sylvia always kept a metal tin filled with this delicious cookie. When we were children, she used to serve them to my cousins Nadine, Bobby, and me with warm coffee-milk that was poured into clear glass cups.

8 heaping tablespoons vegetable shortening
1 cup sugar
2 eggs
1 teaspoon vanilla
3 cups flour, unbleached and presifted
2 teaspoons baking powder
  pinch of salt

Preheat oven to 350°.   Makes 2 dozen.

Cream shortening and sugar together. Add remaining ingredients and mix well. Place dough in pastry bag fitted with star-shape attachment. Press 3-inch long strips onto baking sheet. Bake for 12-15 minutes until golden brown.

POPPY SEED COOKIES (P)

The Yiddish name is Muhn Kichel but I used to call them "Bubbie Cookies." They are the cookies my Bubbie always made for family gatherings.

1/2 cup poppy seeds
  4 cups flour, unbleached and presifted
  1 teaspoon baking powder
  1 cup sugar plus additional 1/2 cup for sprinkling
  3 large eggs, beaten
1/2 cup canola oil
1/4 cup orange juice
  1 teaspoon vanilla extract

Preheat oven to 350°.   Makes 3 dozen.

Continued on next page.

Combine dry ingredients and mix well. Combine eggs with oil, juice, and vanilla and beat thoroughly with a whisk. Add to dry ingredients and knead to make soft dough.

Divide dough into three portions and flatten. On floured board with floured rolling pin, roll to 1/8 inch thickness. Cut with 2-1/2 inch cookie cutter. Place on greased baking sheet and sprinkle well with sugar. Bake for 12-15 minutes until browned. Unbaked, divided dough can be wrapped in plastic wrap and frozen.

LIME, SOUR CREAM DESSERT MOLD (M)

2 packages kosher lime gelatin
1 cup boiling water
1 14-ounce can crushed pineapple, in own juice, not drained
1 pint sour cream
1 6-ounce jar maraschino cherries, drained and quartered
1/2 cup coarsely chopped walnuts

8 servings.

In a large bowl, dissolve gelatin in boiling water. Cool until syrupy like egg whites. Add crushed pineapple with its juice. Beat in sour cream until smooth. Add nuts and cherries.

Pour into a well oiled 2-quart mold. Chill until set. Invert onto serving dish.

MANDARIN ORANGE SHERBET DESSERT MOLD (M)

2 small packages kosher orange gelatin
2 cups boiling water
1 11-ounce can mandarin oranges, drained; reserve liquid
1 pint orange sherbet, softened

8 servings.

In a large bowl, dissolve gelatin in boiling water.

Drain oranges into a measuring cup. Add enough water to equal 1 cup. Add boiling water to gelatin and stir to dissolve. Add juice mixture and stir. Chill until slightly thickened. With electric beaters, blend in sherbet and mandarin oranges. Pour into a 1-1/2 quart mold. Chill until firm. Invert onto serving dish.

CUSTARD BREAD PUDDING (M)

4 cups sourdough bread cubes, toasted
1/3 cup each dark and golden raisins
4 cups milk
2/3 cup sugar
8 large eggs, beaten
1 teaspoon ground cinnamon
1 teaspoon ground nutmeg
1 teaspoon vanilla extract

Preheat oven to 325°.   12 servings.

Spray a 10" x 10" baking pan with non-stick baking spray. Cut toasted bread slices into 1-inch cubes and place in pan. Sprinkle raisins over the bread.

In a mixing bowl beat together eggs, milk, sugar, cinnamon, nutmeg, and vanilla. Pour mixture over bread and raisins. Bake for 40 to 45 minutes or until a knife inserted near the center comes out clean. Cool slightly. Serve warm with heavy or whipped cream, if desired.

PAULA'S RICE PUDDING (M)

1-1/2 cups long grain rice, uncooked
(Unbelievable but correct!)
1/4 pound butter
2 large eggs, slightly beaten
3 cups milk
1 12-ounce can evaporated milk
1-1/2 cups sugar
1 cup raisins (optional)
1 tablespoon vanilla flavoring
1 tablespoon cinnamon

Makes 8 cups.

Cook rice according to package directions. Add butter, eggs, both milks, and sugar and cook to boiling. Add vanilla and cinnamon and continue to cook 2 to 3 more minutes. Soak raisins in hot water until plump, then drain; add to rice pudding. Pudding will be thin, but will thicken as it cools. Cool thoroughly and serve at room temperature or chilled. Serve with whipped cream.

FRESH WHIPPED CREAM (M)

1 cup whipping cream
1 tablespoon sugar

1/2 teaspoon vanilla extract

Combine whipping cream, sugar, and vanilla. Beat on medium speed until soft peaks form.

To flavor whipped cream:

Add one of the following ingredients to the vanilla:

✿ 3 tablespoons unsweetened cocoa powder plus 1 more tablespoon sugar.
✿ 2 tablespoons Amaretto, hazelnut, orange, or praline liqueur.
✿ 1 teaspoon instant coffee crystals.
✿ 1/2 teaspoon finely grated lemon, orange, or lime peel.
✿ 1/4 teaspoon ground cinnamon, nutmeg, or ginger.

SUFGANIYOT (DOUGHNUTS) (M)

At Hanukkah-time in Spain and Morocco, a rolled donut that has a sugar glaze called Fichuelas de Hanukkah is eaten. In Israel, a raised jelly donut called Sufganiyot is served.

1	package dry yeast
1/4	cup warm water
2-1/2	cups flour, unbleached and presifted
3/4	cup lukewarm milk
1/2	cup sugar; reserve 2 tablespoons
2	large egg yolks, beaten
1-1/2	tablespoons butter or margarine
1	quart canola oil
	pinch salt
	pinch cinnamon
	jam of your choice (I like apricot or strawberry)

Makes 30.

Proof yeast by dissolving it in the water with reserved 2 tablespoons of sugar. Allow yeast to proof for 5 minutes, until foamy.

Place flour in a bowl, make a well, add yeast mixture, milk, salt, cinnamon, remaining sugar, and egg yolks. Knead until dough has an elastic consistency. If too sticky, add more flour, a tablespoon at a time.

Place dough into a greased bowl, cover and allow to rise for 2 hours. Punch down. Roll dough out to 1/4" on a floured surface. Cut 2" rounds with biscuit cutter. Cover and set aside for 15 minutes.

Heat oil to 375° in a large, deep pot. Drop dough into pot, 3 or 4 at a time. Turn when golden brown. Fry on second side, remove from oil and drain on paper towels.

Fill sufganiyot by inserting a jam filled teaspoon in the top of the doughnut. Distribute jam evenly inside doughnut and carefully remove spoon. Roll in granulated or confectioners' sugar and serve while they are hot.

COCO CHOCO HALVAH (P)

This candy does not taste like the Joyva brand Halvah that I have eaten for most of my life. However, it is excellent and gives me a joyful feeling and makes me want to sing and dance! Most of these ingredients can be found in health food stores.

1/3 cup unsweetened coconut, finely shredded
1/3 cup rolled oats
1/4 cup sunflower seeds, unsalted
  3 tablespoons tahini (sesame paste), well stirred
  3 tablespoons honey
  2 tablespoons dark carob or cocoa powder
1/4 teaspoon ground cinnamon
1/4 cup sesame seeds, unsalted

Makes about 40 pieces.

In a food processor fitted with a steel blade, process coconut, oats, and sunflower seeds until powdery.

In a mixing bowl combine tahini, honey, carob powder, and cinnamon. Add coconut mixture and stir with a wooden spoon. Knead with your hands until smooth. Add honey or tahini, 1 tablespoon at a time, if too dry.

Roll into a ball; press to 1 inch height and form a rectangular shape. Roll in sesame seeds to cover. Wrap in plastic wrap and refrigerate for about 3 hours, until firm. Slice into 1-inch pieces and serve.

PAREVE MACAROONS (P)

3-1/2 ounces sweetened, shredded coconut
  1/3 cup sugar
1-1/2 tablespoons potato starch
  1/8 teaspoon salt
    2 egg whites, stiffly beaten
  1/2 teaspoon almond extract
  1/2 cup miniature chocolate morsels (optional)

Preheat oven to 325°.   Makes 12.

Combine coconut, sugar, potato starch, and salt.

Fold in egg whites, chocolate chips, and almond extract. Drop by teaspoon onto lightly greased baking sheets. Bake for 10 minutes or until golden brown.

DAIRY MACAROONS (M)

  1 14-ounce can sweetened shredded coconut
2/3 cup sweetened condensed milk
1/4 cup farmer cheese or large curd cottage cheese, drained

Preheat oven to 350°.   Makes 36.

Mash cottage cheese and stir together with milk and coconut. Mix thoroughly. Drop by tablespoon onto buttered baking sheet.

Squeeze each macaroon so it holds together then press with a fork to flatten slightly.

Bake for 15 minutes. Cool and serve. Refrigerate to store.

CHEESECAKE PIE (M)

3 8-ounce packages cream cheese, softened
3/4 cup sugar
3/4 teaspoon vanilla extract
3 large eggs, beaten
2 cups fresh strawberries, sliced

Preheat oven to 350°.   8 servings.

Mix cream cheese, sugar, and vanilla with electric mixer on medium speed until well blended. Add eggs, 1 at a time, mixing on low speed after each addition, just until blended. Pour over crust.

Bake for 50 minutes or until center is almost set. Refrigerate 4 hours or overnight. Top with fresh strawberries, prepared fruit filling, preserves, or melted chocolate.

MACAROON CRUST

3 cups soft coconut macaroon crumbs
3 tablespoons butter or margarine, melted

Mix together crumbs and butter. Press onto bottom and sides of 10" pie pan, or line miniature muffin tins with paper cups and sprinkle mixture on bottom.

GRAHAM CRACKER CRUST

1-1/2 cups graham cracker crumbs
1/4 cup butter, melted
3 tablespoons brown sugar
1 teaspoon cinnamon

Toss together graham cracker crumbs, brown sugar, butter, and cinnamon. Press on bottom and sides of 10" pie pan, or line miniature muffin tins with paper cups and sprinkle mixture on bottom.

POOKIE COOKIES (P)

2   egg whites, beaten
1/8 teaspoon salt
1   teaspoon vanilla extract
1/2 cup sugar
1   cup chocolate chips, chopped walnuts, or raisins

Preheat oven to 300°.   Makes 24.

Beat the egg whites until foamy. Add salt and continue beating egg whites until stiff but not dry. Add vanilla and gradually beat in sugar until stiff and satiny. Fold in chocolate chips. Drop by teaspoonful on greased baking sheet. Bake for 22-25 minutes.

CRUNCHY COOKIES WITH RAISINS (P)

2   cups matzo meal
2   cups matzo farfel
1   cup sugar
3/4 cup brown sugar
1/2 cup walnuts or pecans
2/3 cup canola oil
4   large eggs, beaten*
2   teaspoons cinnamon
1/2 teaspoon salt
1/2 cup raising

Preheat oven to 350°.   Makes 3-4 dozen.

Place matzo meal, farfel, and sugars in food processor that has been fitted with steel blade and lightly pulse process until farfel is like coarse meal. Pour mixture into a large mixing bowl.

Chop nuts in food processor and pour into bowl with matzo mixture. In food processor, combine oil, eggs, cinnamon, and salt; add to dry ingredients and mix well. Stir in raisins. Drop by teaspoon on greased baking sheet, 2 inches apart. Bake 30 to 35 minutes until browned.

*For a softer cookie, add an extra egg.

PASSOVER SPONGE CAKE (P)

12 large eggs, separated
1-3/4 cups sugar
1/2 cup potato starch
3 heaping tablespoons cake meal, sifted
1-1/2 teaspoons lemon rind
4-1/2 tablespoons lemon juice

Do not preheat oven.   12 servings.

In a large mixing bowl, beat the egg yolks very well. Gradually add 1-1/2 cups of the sugar and continue beating until blended.

Fold sifted cake meal and potato starch into the yolk mixture. Add the juice and lemon rind. Beat the egg whites until stiff and slowly add remaining 1/4 cup sugar.

Fold the egg whites into the yolk mixture. Pour batter into a 10-inch tube pan and place in a cold oven. Bake for 1 hour at 350°. Invert cake onto a cake rack to cool.

APPLE AND NUT CHARLOTTE (P)

2 large sweet apples, pared and diced
5 large eggs, separated
1 cup chopped walnuts
1/4 cup honey
1/2 teaspoon salt
2 tablespoons sugar
1 tablespoon lemon juice
1 tablespoon grated lemon rind

Preheat oven to 350°.   9 servings.

Line bottom of greased 9" x 9" pan with apple slices. Beat egg yolks until light and frothy. Add nuts, honey, salt, sugar, juice, and rind. Blend well. Beat egg whites until stiff, but not dry. Fold into mixture. Pour over apple slices. Bake 30 minutes or until set.

KUGELHOPF (M)

This jelly-roll is used to break the fast on Yom Kippur in Hungary. Although many of the ingredients are used in some kugels, it is definitely not a kugel. I love the name!

Dough:

    1 ounce active dry yeast
    6 cups flour, presifted and unbleached
2-1/2 cups sugar
    2 cups milk, heated to 120°
    1 teaspoon salt
1-1/4 cups butter
    3 egg yolks
    1 whole egg, beaten
      vanilla powdered sugar (p. 245), enough for sprinkling

Heat milk to lukewarm. Combine yeast, 2 tablespoons of the flour, 1 teaspoon of the sugar, and milk and stir until smooth. Cover with a towel and set aside to rise. Cream butter and remaining sugar. Add egg yolks and beat. Place remaining flour and salt in large bowl. Form well in center and pour in yeast and egg mixtures. Beat with dough hooks on electric mixer until dough comes loose from sides and bottom of bowl. Cover with towel and set in unheated oven to rise until doubled, about 1 hour.

Filling:

    2 tablespoons butter, melted   3-1/2 tablespoons sugar
1/2 cup white raisins   1 tablespoon cinnamon
    1 teaspoon each vanilla, orange, and lemon extract

Preheat oven to 350°.   10 servings.

Combine filling ingredients. Place dough on floured board and knead well. With floured rolling pin, roll to 1/4-inch thickness. Spread with filling mixture and roll, jelly-roll fashion, from long end. Brush with beaten egg and sprinkle with vanilla powdered sugar. Bake for 1 hour.

HOLIDAYS AND MENUS

TRADITIONAL MEAT MENU
FOR A HOLIDAY OR
FRIDAY NIGHT SABBATH

Gefilte fish with horseradish or
Chopped liver

Chicken soup with matzo balls, noodles, or kreplach

Chicken or brisket
Potato kugel or other pareve kugel
Knishes or stuffed kishka (derma)
Glazed carrots or green vegetable
Cucumber, Tomato, and Green Pepper Salad
Hallah
Traditional Sweet Wine

Fruit
Honey Cake
Strudel, Mandelbroit, Tayglach
Coffee or tea

TRADITIONAL ASHKENAZIC MENU
FOR SATURDAY SABBATH NOON MEAL

Fruit salad
Cholent and Cholent Kugel

YOM HA'ATZMAUT AND YOM YERUSHALAYIM
Israel Independence Day and Jerusalem Day
5th of Iyar and 15th of Iyar

YOM YERUSHALAYIM MENU

Hummus
Falafel
Cucumber, Tomato, and Bell Pepper Salad
Tabouleh
Eggplant Salad or Baba Ganoush
Tahini Dip
Pita Bread
Jerusalem Kugel

TU B'SHVAT
15th of Shvat

The New Year for Trees

TU B'SHVAT MENU

Fruit salad
Nuts
Dates
Figs
Pomegranate
Halvah
Wine

PURIM
14th of Adar

Purim is often considered a holiday for the children, even though its message of political manipulation and ultimate deliverance is an important story for all. On this day the story is read from the Scroll of Esther, the Megillah. Persian Jews were triumphant over Haman, an ambitious and evil minister. He gained power by taking advantage of King Ahasuerus, who was easily influenced. The King ordered everyone to bow down to Haman but a Jewish man named Mordecai refused. Haman ordered the King to kill him and all Jews on a date that would be determined by casting "lots" or, in Hebrew, Purim.

Queen Esther, who was loved by everyone, was Jewish and Mordecai's cousin. However, the King and Haman did not know this. When she learned about the plot, she prepared a great feast for Haman and the King. She told the King that Haman wanted to have her and all of her people killed. Realizing that Haman was truly an evil man, the King had Haman hung in the gallows that was prepared for Mordecai.

The holiday is celebrated with festive carnivals where people, young and old, dress in costumes and twirl groggers (noise makers). Games and food are included in the celebration. It is one of the few occasions when an abundance of wine is permitted to be consumed. "One should drink enough wine on Purim so as not to be able to distinguish between the names of Mordecai and Haman." Triangular shaped foods are served to remind us of Haman's hat, in Hebrew "Hamantashen." In Israel a filled cookie called Aznei Haman, meaning Haman's ears, are served.

PURIM MENU

Chicken in Red Wine
Triangular shaped
Kreplach
Hallah
Hamantashen

PASSOVER
15th of Nissan

The month of Nissan is associated with redemption. The first night of Passover (Pesach) is celebrated on the night of the spring full moon —the "birthday" of the Jewish Nation.

When the Israelites where shepherds they celebrated the coming of spring. They became farmers when they settled in Canaan, and spring became even more important. During this eight-day holiday, God is thanked for things that grow and for new birth. We celebrate with friends and family our freedom from winter, and that we can again plant and grow crops. We also celebrate our history.

Every year, for the last 3,000 years, Jews worldwide have recounted the powerful story of Passover. During an in-the-home religious service that is called a Seder, we read from a book that is called a Haggadah. It tells about our slavery in Egypt, and about Moses, and the Exodus. It reminds us that no person is truly free when another is enslaved, in fear, hungry, or the victim of prejudice. On this holiday, we are also reminded of our dependence on God and that we should be humble.

THE PASSOVER MEAL

After the first part of the Seder, dinner is served. The appetizer, soup, main course, and dessert are usually traditional foods. Roasted meat is not usually served on a Seder night because of its resemblance to the Pesach sacrifice. During the following days of Passover, roasted lamb is frequently served, especially by Sephardic Jews. Root vegetables, such as potatoes and onions, which grew quickly in the Diaspora during the sojourn out of Egypt, are used.
Matzo (unleavened bread) and four cups of wine are referred to and consumed during the Passover Seder ritual. Matzo is eaten at meals throughout the holiday.

PASSOVER MENU

Gefilte Fish with Horseradish
Chopped Liver

Chicken Soup with Matzo Balls

Chicken with Oranges, Apricots, and
Almonds

Passover Spinach Kugel
Freshly Steamed Asparagus

Phyllis's Popovers
Matzo

Sweet Kosher Wine

Macaroons
Sponge Cake
Pookie Cookies

Hot Tea

 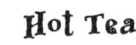 

ON THE SEDER PLATE...

...symbolic foods are placed, and they are referred to and tasted during the Seder. A lamb bone and roasted egg are only displayed; the other foods are both displayed and eaten.

ZEROAH (shank bone) BAYTZAH (roasted egg)

KARPAS (mild green vegetable) HAROSET (mortar)

MORAR (bitter herbs) CHAZERET (another herb)*

* The Bible indicates that more than one herb should be used for Passover. Therefore, radish, celery, or another green vegetable can be used in addition to the morar.

THE HAROSET

Four of the six foods on the ceremonial Seder plate are passed to everyone at the table and eaten at the appropriate time during the Seder. Haroset is one of those foods. It symbolizes the mortar that our forebears used to build Pharaoh's cities. Leftovers are a wonderful treat throughout the holiday.

ASHKENAZIC HAROSET (P)

4 medium sweet apples, with skin and coarsely chopped
1 cup chopped walnuts
2 teaspoons honey (optional)
1/2 teaspoon cinnamon
3 tablespoons sweet Passover Concord grape wine

Combine everything and store in covered container in refrigerator. Serve cold.

SEPHARDIC HAROSET (P)

6 large calimyrna dried figs
6 pitted dates
2 tablespoons sesame seeds
1 teaspoon honey
1/2 teaspoon ground ginger
1/8 teaspoon ground coriander seeds

Finely chop dates and figs with steel blade in food processor. Mix in sesame seeds, honey, ginger, and coriander. Store in refrigerator, tightly covered, for up to 2 weeks. Bring to room temperature before serving.

SHIFIRAH B'OMER
16TH OF NISSAN

AND

LAG B'OMER
18th of Iyar

On the second day of Passover, we begin to celebrate the start of the grain harvest by "Counting the Omer," in Hebrew *"Sefirah B'Omer."* On this day, long ago, a sheaf (omer) of barley, was brought to the Holy Temple in Jerusalem and was symbolically given in thanks.

About sixty years after the destruction of the Second Holy Temple in Jerusalem, around 130 CE, Shimon Bar Kochba and his followers rebelled against the Romans in an effort to regain national independence. He and Rabbi Akiva (spiritual leader of the Jews) were killed as well as thousands of the rabbi's students and disciples. On the thirty-third day of the Counting of the Omer (Lag B'Omer), the Jews were miraculously, although briefly, successful in defeating their enemy. On that day, people have festive picnics and barbeque gatherings complete with games and races.

DAIRY PICNIC MENU

Tuna Sandwiches
Salads
Watermelon
Cool Whip Jygunda Kugel

SHAVUOT
6th of Sivan

The holiday of Shavuot begins forty-nine days after the start of Sefirah B'Omer. On this day, two loaves of bread made from the first grains (omer) were given as an offering in the Holy Temple.

The "countdown" during the holiday of Sefirah B'Omer shows the connection between the two holidays of Passover and Shavuot. This holiday celebrates the "Giving of the Law" (Torah). "Our freedom from slavery was not complete until we received the Torah."

Dairy meals are usually served, possibly as a reminder of the time right after the Torah was received when the Israelites were not yet sure of the laws of kosher slaughtering. In place of meat, they ate dairy meals.

SHAVUOT MENU

Traditional Dairy Meal Menu
Blintz Soufflé
Cheese kugel topped with fruit
Cheese Pie

SUKKOT
15th of Tishrei

Before the seven-day holiday of Sukkot (the Festival of the Fall Harvest, also called the Feast of Tabernackles), Sukkahs made of vines and dried leaves are set up. A large variety of fruits and vegetables are used to decorate. Sukkahs are a reminder of the small huts that the harvesters and ancient Israelites lived in during their sojourn in the wilderness.

During the holiday, we eat meals and snacks in the Sukkah, unless it rains. Candles are lit and we give thanks for a bountiful harvest with prayers. The mitzvah (good deed) of etrog and lulav, which are used during the religious service, represents the concept of unity amongst the Jewish people, regardless of their differences.

Etrog is a sweet smelling fruit that resembles a lemon, and lulav is a palm frond combined with a myrtle branch and a willow. They represent people who are learned and those who are not learned in Torah, and those who perform good deeds and people who do not. We recall that we cannot reach our true potential if we are not united and do not rely on the help of others.

SUKKOT MENU

Gedempt
Hallah
Honey
Dried Fruit and Nut Mix Kugel

SIMCHAT TORAH
23rd of Tishrei

Simchat Torah marks the completion of the Torah cycle. Synagogues hold festive services full of song, fun, and dancing with the Torahs. Stuffed cabbage, rolled into the shape of Torah scrolls is often served. Baked potato latkes, knishes, and cookies can also be fashioned as Torahs, or decorate a sweet kugel with fruit in the shaped of a Torah.

SIMCHAT TORAH MENU

Stuffed Cabbage
Knishes
Kugel
Tossed salad
Schnecken
Cookies

ROSH HASHANAH
1st of Tishrei

Rosh Hashanah means "head of the year," and the holiday celebrates the Jewish New Year. During this holiday, symbolic foods are eaten in the hope that the year will bring good luck, sweetness, wisdom, fertility, prosperity, and freedom from sin and sadness.

FOOD SYMBOLISM FOR THIS HOLIDAY

Foods that are eaten:

Honey — Used in many ways to symbolize the hope that our lives will be sweet in the coming year:

> Apple slices and chunks of hallah are dipped in honey.
> Kugel sweetened with honey is served as a side dish.
> Honey cake is usually included as dessert.

Dates — The Hebrew word for dates (*tamar*), sounds like part of a blessing in which we ask to be cleansed of sin. They are also eaten because they are sweet and symbols of peace and beauty.

Hallah — For this holiday it is fashioned into a circular shape to symbolize a long span of life and a well rounded year. The spiral would be higher in the center representing "the ascent to heaven."

Gefilte Fish — Eating fish is a token of wisdom, fortune, and fertility.

Carrots — The Yiddish word "mehren" can mean either "carrots" or "increase" and carrots represent the desire that our virtues will be increased. When cut into thin, round slices, carrots look like coins. They symbolize increase in numbers and wealth.

Kreplach – The chopped meat filling is symbolic of the traditional flogging men may receive on the night before (*erev*) Yom Kippur, when they ask forgiveness for their sins.

Foods that are not eaten:

Because this is a joyful holiday, we should not be reminded of sadness or bitterness by eating foods that are bitter, sour, or black.

Nuts — According to Kabbalah, the numerical value of the letters in the Hebrew word for nut (egoz) is close to that of the word for sin (chet) when spelled without the letter "aleph." Both words "equal" seventeen.

YOM KIPPUR
10th of Tishrei

Yom Kippur, the "Day of Atonement," is the most solemn holiday of the Jewish calendar. This is a day of fasting when we are supposed to feel the pain of hunger and be aware of how hard it is to atone for our sins. In addition to abstaining from food, drinking any liquid during the fast is also prohibited. However, people who are sick, under the age of thirteen, pregnant, or nursing do not have to fast.

A feast before the fast takes place in the evening before Yom Kippur. Foods prepared should not be highly salted or spiced, so that people will not become too thirsty while fasting. Boiled chicken that is used to prepare chicken soup is sometimes served as the main course with a vegetable and a pareve kugel as side dishes.

It has become a tradition in this country to serve a dairy meal that includes smoked fish, bagels, and dairy kugel to break the fast.

TRADITIONAL DAIRY MEAL
MENU FOR A CROWD

If you start early, this meal could last all day! Serve with dairy noodle kugel (fruity or not), knishes, and blintzes.

Fish: Kippered salmon, nova and/or belly lox, sable, chubs, white fish

      Herring: Pickled, plain, in cream sauce, schmaltz, chopped

      Fish   Tuna, salmon, white fish,
      Salad: kosher mock seafood

Cheese: Cream cheese, cottage cheese, Muenster, American, Swiss

Creams: Sour cream, half and half

Butter: Sweet, lightly salted

Fruits: Assorted whole fresh fruit, fruit salad

Veggies: Cold sliced cucumbers, onions, tomatoes

Breads: Bagels (assorted), rye bread (plain and seeded), pumpernickel or black bread

Desserts: Kosher Jell-O molds, strudel, apple cake, rugala, schnecken, and mandelbroit, kugelhopf (jelly roll)

Beverages: Coffee, tea, soda, water, seltzer, milk, punch

HANUKKAH
25th of Kislev

About 2,100 years ago, under the leadership of Judah Maccabee, the Maccabean army was victorious over the Syrians. When the people of Judea were about to light the menorah to rededicate the Temple, legend tells only one small cruse of oil was found — enough for just one day. However, a miracle happened and the oil lasted eight days, long enough for new holy olive-oil to be pressed.

Jews celebrate Hanukkah, the Festival of Lights, for that reason. The word Hanukkah means dedication. The holiday has been celebrated since 165 BCE and lasts for eight days. A menorah called a *"Hanukkiah"* is used. A new candle is added each day, from right to left, and lit from left to right by a "servant" candle called a *"shammas"* until all eight are aglow. After lighting the candles while chanting a prayer, songs are sung and presents are opened. Games are played with a four-sided top called a *"dreidel."*

Eating food that has been prepared in oil during Hanukkah is a tradition for Jews in many parts of the world. It is a reminder of the miracle that happened when the Temple in Jerusalem was rededicated. In Spain and Morocco, a rolled donut that has a sugar glaze called Fichuelas de Hanukkah is eaten. In Israel, a raised jelly donut called *"sufganiyot"* is served at Hanukkah time.

HANUKKAH DINNER MENU

Hot Cabbage Borscht
Roasted chicken
Steve's Potato Latkes
Steamed whole green beans and sliced mushrooms
Sufganiyot

HANUKKAH PARTY MENU

Mini Potato Kugels made in muffin pans and/or
Latkes — a variety or just potato
Applesauce and/or Sugar for topping

Sliced meats including:
Turkey, Roast Beef, Corned Beef, Pastrami

Real (imitations will not do) hard crusted, sliced
Jewish Rye, Pumpernickel, and Rolls

Cole slaw
Pickles and olives
Sliced assorted vegetables
Mayonnaise, Russian dressing, ketchup, mustard

Mandelbroit, Strudel, Hanukkah Cookies, and
Chocolate Hanukkah Gelt

JEWISH CALENDAR

The Jewish calendar is primarily lunar. Each month begins on the new moon, when a sliver of moon becomes visible after the dark moon.

There are approximately 12.4 lunar months in every 12-month solar year. Therefore a 12-month lunar calendar looses about 11 days every year and a 13-month lunar gains 19 days every year. To compensate for the "drift," a second month of Adar is added in a 19-year cycle. This occurs on the 3rd, 6th, 8th, 11th, 14th, 17th, and 19th year. The current cycle began in the Jewish year 5758, October 2, 1997.

Although Nissan is the first month, the number of the year changes in the 7th month (Tishri) when we celebrate the holiday of *Rosh Hashanna* (head of the year).

Hebrew Month	Duration	Gregorian Month
Nissan	30 days	March-April
Iyar	29 days	April-May
Sivan	30 days	May-June
Tammuz	29 days	June-July
Av	30 days	July-August
Elul	29 days	July-August
Tishri	30 days	September-October
Cheshvan	29 or 30 days	October-November
Kislev	29 or 30 days	November-December
Tevet	29 days	December-January
Shevat	30 days	January-February
Adar	29 or 30 days	February-March
AdarII	29 days	March-April

241

HINTS

1. Individual servings — Bake small portions of kugel in muffin tins for 1/4 less time than what is called for in recipe or until mixture is set.

2. Read entire recipe before starting to prepare and prepare as written.

3. Noodle cooking — To prevent noodles from sticking together, add 1 tablespoon of oil to the water. Run water through the noodles after draining.

4. Pot lids — Remove the lid of a steaming pot by tilting it away from your face.

5. Cottage cheese — Cottage cheese will last longer in refrigerator if you "burp" the air out as you would with a plastic storage container. Turn the container upside down and return to the refrigerator. This will prevent air from touching the cheese and it will keep far longer than if stored upright.

6. Butter —Butter will soften quickly if you grate it while hard and cold, or microwave at 30% power for 1 minute.

7. Cream cheese — Cream cheese will soften quickly microwaved at 30% power for 2 to 2-1/2 minutes for 8 ounces. A 3-ounce package will soften in 1-1/2 to 2 minutes.

8. Onion chopping — Prevent tears by running onion under cold water while peeling.

9. Chopping and grating — Use the food processor — it's fabulous! However, for dicing (larger pieces), use a knife.

10. Save a pot — Melt butter or margarine in the same pan you will be baking in.

11. Cabbage odor — To absorb cabbage-cooking odor, place a small tin cup or can half-filled with vinegar on stove or counter near where cabbage will be cooking.

12. Brown sugar — Brown sugar will not harden if dried fruit such as prunes are placed in the container. If it hardens, microwave for 1-2 minutes on low setting.

13. Grater cleaning — Use a toothbrush to clean lemon rind, cheese, onion, etc. out of grater before washing it.

14. Separating eggs — You can remove egg yolk that has gotten into the white while separating eggs by dipping a piece of the shell into the bowl. Yolk will just slide right onto it. Of course, if your problem is that a piece of shell has fallen into your egg white, lots of luck getting it out — it is not as easy.

15. Buying and storing eggs — Never buy eggs that have not been refrigerated and be sure to put them into your refrigerator as soon as possible. They should be stored in their own carton with the pointed end down so that they will not lose vitamins. They will keep for 4 to 5 weeks. Raw egg whites keep a week to 10 days if refrigerated in a tightly covered container.

16. Egg whites — Egg whites can be frozen in ice cube trays and defrosted as needed. Refrigerate unbroken raw egg yolks covered with water in a tightly covered container. Drain and use within 2 to 3 days. Always use a glass bowl when whipping egg whites, not plastic, metal, or wood.

17. Potatoes — To prevent potatoes from turning black, place pared potatoes in a bowl of water with some lemon juice added.

18. Cutting boards — Use non-absorbent cutting boards for meat. Rub a cut lemon on a wooden board to remove onion scent.

19. Yeast — Proof 1 package of dry active yeast by adding 1 teaspoon of sugar and 1/4 cup of water. If the yeast does not get foamy, throw it away and get a different package. The first one may have expired.

20. Chicken soup fat — To remove, place chicken and vegetables in one container and broth in another. Refrigerate overnight and the fat will solidify at the top of the now jellied broth. Take it away!

FOOD SUBSTITUTIONS

WHITE SUGAR

Substitute 1 cup of sugar with:

  1 cup honey
1/2 cup apple, white grape, orange, or pineapple juice
     concentrate.
1/2 cup molasses
  1 cup Sucanat
2/3 cup maple syrup
  2 medium bananas, mashed
3/4 cup brown sugar
    1 cup sugar-free and "in their own juices" canned and
     puréed fruit, jams, and jellies.

OR: Heat-stable sugar substitutes. Use the manufacturer's equivalent of what your recipe calls for in sugar. Sugar substitutes that contain Nutrasweet are not heat-stable and they lose their sweetness when baked for a long time.

Use half white sugar and make up difference in taste using sugar substitute to cut calories and keep the sugar taste.

Reduce amount of sugar that recipe calls for by 1/4 in baked goods and desserts and substitute flour for omitted sugar.

VANILLA POWDERED SUGAR

Place powdered sugar in a jar with a vanilla bean and cover tightly. Let stand overnight. Makes a wonderful topping when sprinkled on sweet kugel, cakes, and cookies.

FATS

Canola (highest in beneficial monounsaturated fat) and corn oils have low levels of saturated (bad) fatty acids and are rich sources of vitamin E.

Olive oil (also monounsaturated) has a more robust taste. There are many varieties of olive oil. Cold-pressed extra virgin is the best. Do not use this oil for baking cakes, muffins, cookies, piecrust, or bread.

Vegetable oil may contain tropical oils (i.e. coconut) and may be high in saturated fats.

Baking substitutions for fat. Add with liquid ingredients. *

✿ Replace with unsweetened applesauce or puréed fruit (such as baby food). Puréed prunes good w/chocolate.
✿ Replace with unsweetened apple butter, unsweetened pumpkin butter, or orange juice. Use non-stick cooking or baking spray for greasing pans.
✿ Use low calorie mayonnaise.
✿ Reduce fat by 1/3 in quick breads, muffins, and cookies.

* Consistency of baked goods may be denser when making substitutions. Beat egg whites and fold into batter, and use cake flour.

Sautéing and browning substitutions for fat:

✿ Use a non-stick cooking or baking spray to grease your pans.
✿ Steam vegetables in water instead of sautéing in oil.
✿ 3 tablespoons of flat beer for every tablespoon butter.
✿ 3 tablespoons of wine for every tablespoon of butter.

Margarine — Soft tub margarine is higher in (good) polyunsaturates than the hardened variety. Light corn or canola oil margarine is OK for spreads or kugel, but not for cakes, cookies, and pastries.

Butter — Light butter contains half the fat of butter or margarine and is low in sodium and cholesterol. Do not substitute oil for butter when baking cookies, cakes, dairy kugel, and pastries. However, butter can be substituted for solid shortening. Use health food store nutritional yeast on popcorn.

CLARIFIED BUTTER, BUTTER OIL, OR GHEE

Also called anhydrous milk-fat, this is butter without milk solids and is preferred for preparing foods that need to be sautéed over a high heat, like omelets, fish, and potatoes. It does not smoke and will not go rancid.

To prepare: Melt 1 pound of butter, cut in small pieces, in a small saucepan, using very low heat. Water will evaporate and a white milky residue will form on the bottom of the saucepan. Skim off the foam that rises to the surface, and pour the clear, melted butter off the milk residue. Store in glass jar with tightly fitting lid.

EGGS

Some of the recipes in this book may appear to be less healthy than they actually are. For instance, a kugel that is made with 10 eggs may yield 24 servings. Therefore, each serving would only contain slightly less than 1/2 an egg. Large eggs contain 210 milligrams of cholesterol and are 96% free of saturated fat. 3 to 4 large or 4 to 5 medium whole eggs per week are recommended for the average diet. According to the United States Department of Agriculture, eggs are an important part of a healthy diet. They are nutrient-dense, provide essential vitamins and minerals, and are economical, low-calorie, and a source of high-quality protein. They contain mono-unsaturated fat, which research suggests is healthful.

If you want or need to cut back on your egg intake, for every whole egg, you can substitute the following for each whole egg:

2 egg whites OR
3 tablespoons of commercial egg substitute.

DAIRY PRODUCTS

For lower fat and cholesterol, substitute the foods listed below. However, recipes may taste slightly blander and consistency may be different than if recipe is prepared as originally stated.

Substitute:

Milk:	skim or low-fat (2 percent).
Sour cream:	light sour cream or yogurt
Cottage cheese:	low-fat cottage cheese
Cream cheese:	light cream cheese, farmer cheese, imitation cream cheese, low-fat cottage cheese, part skim ricotta, nonfat yogurt cheese.*

*How to make yogurt cheese or to drain cottage cheese:

Use coffee filter in strainer positioned over bowl. Pour nonfat yogurt into filter and let drain overnight in the refrigerator. Do not allow strainer to touch whey.

EQUIVALENTS

ABBREVIATIONS

tsp. = teaspoon	pt. = pint	oz. = ounces	sm. = small
tbsp. = tablespoon	qt. = quart	lb. = pound	med. = medium
c. = cup			lg. = large

WEIGHTS AND MEASURES

1 tablespoon	=	3 teaspoons
1/8 cup	=	1 ounce or 2 tablespoons
1/4 cup	=	4 tablespoons
1/3 cup	=	5 tablespoons + 1 teaspoon
1/2 cup	=	8 tablespoons
4 ounces	=	1/4 pound dry or 1/2 cup liquid
8 ounces	=	1/2 pound dry or 1 cup liquid
16 ounces	=	1 pound dry, 2 cups liquid or 1 pint
32 ounces	=	2 pound dry, 4 cups liquid or 1 quart
Dash		= a few shakes or 8 drops
Pinch		= amount that can be taken between thumb and finger
Some and a little		= a pinch or a dash

Apples	1 pound	= 3 medium; 3 cups sliced
Butter/margarine	1 stick	= 1/2 cup; 1/4 pound; 8 tablespoons
Carrots	3 or 4	= 3 cups
Corn Flakes	3 cups dry, whole'	= 1 cup dry, crushed
Cottage Cheese	1/2 pound	= 1 cup; 8 ounces
Cream Cheese	3 ounces	= 6 tablespoons
Eggs, whole	5 large eggs	= 1 cup
	9 medium eggs	= 1 pound
	12 large yolks	= 1 cup
	9 large whites	= 1 cup
	2 whites	= 1 whole egg
Egg substitute	1 portion	= 1 egg
Flour:		
all purpose	1 pound	= 4 cups
	1 ounce	= 4 tablespoons
	1 cup sifted	= 1 cup presifted; 1 cup plus 2 tablespoons cake flour
substitutions for Passover	1 cup	= 1/4 cup matzo meal; 3/4 cup potato starch
	1/2 cup	= 2 tablespoons matzo meal; 6 tablespoons potato starch
Garlic	1 medium clove	= 1/8 teaspoon powder
Herbs, fresh	1 tablespoon	= 1 teaspoon dried
Lemon	1 medium	= 3 tablespoons juice; 1 tablespoon rind
Milk:		
Whole	1 cup	= 1/2 cup evaporated plus 1/2 cup water
buttermilk	1 cup	= 1 cup whole plus 1 tablespoon vinegar; 1 tablespoon lemon juice
Noodles	1 pound raw	= 9 cups cooked

Nuts, in shell:		
almonds	1 pound	= 1/4 pound nutmeat; about 1 cup
pecans	1 pound	= 2-1/4 cups in shell; 4 cups nutmeat
walnuts	1 pound	= 2 cups in shell; 3-1/2 cups nutmeat
Onions	6 or 7 medium	= 2-1/2 cups diced
	1 small	= 1 tablespoon rehydrated, minced
Orange	1 medium	= 1/3 cup juice; 2 tablespoons rind
Peaches	2 pounds	= 2 cups sliced; 8 medium
Potatoes:		
white	1 pound	= 3 medium; 2-1/3 cups sliced
sweet (yams)	1 pound	= 3 medium; 3 cups sliced
Potato flour	1 cup	= 1 cup potato starch
Raisins	1 pound	= 3 cups
Rice	1 cup raw	= 3 cups cooked
Salt	1 teaspoon	= 1 teaspoon light
Schmaltz	1 cup	= 1 cup oil
Sour Cream	1 cup	= 1/3 cup butter plus 2/3 cup buttermilk
Strawberries	1 pint	= 2 cups sliced
Sugar, white	1 pound	= 2-1/4 cups
	1 cup	= 1 cup brown, firmly packed
Vanilla extract	1 teaspoon	= 1 tablespoon imitation vanilla flavoring

250

GLOSSARY

Al dente:	Pasta or vegetables that are cooked slightly underdone. See parboiling.
Bake:	To cook food by dry heat, usually in an oven.
Baste:	To moisten baked or roasted foods with liquid during baking.
Beating:	Mixing or combining with a brisk or rotary motion.
Blanching:	Submerging or dipping in boiling water and then plunging into cold water.
Blend:	To combine by stirring or mixing to a smooth consistency.
Boiling:	Cooking in liquid at boiling temperature (212° Fahrenheit).
Brush:	To spread a thin coating of liquid or semi-liquid over the top.
Caramelize:	To dissolve sugar and water slowly, then heat until it thickens and turns caramel brown.
Chopping:	Cutting into very small pieces with a knife or food-chopper.
Combine:	To mix or blend ingredients.
Cracklings:	The crisp brown pieces that remain when all the fat is rendered from poultry; grebenes.
Creaming:	Stirring or mixing to a smooth and creamy softness.
Cubing:	Cutting into cubes.
Cutting in:	Distributing a creamy mixture through a dry mixture by aid of a cutting motion with a knife, spatula, or pastry blender.
Dash:	A small quantity; several quick shakes of a spice shaker.
Dice:	To cut into very small pieces about 1/2 inch in size.
Dissolve:	To blend a liquid together with solid substance.
Dotting:	Scattering small bits over the surface.
Dough:	A mixture of ingredients including flour and liquid, blended or kneaded smooth enough to form into desired shapes by rolling or patting.
Drain:	To remove liquid from solids by pouring through a colander or sieve.
Drizzle:	To slowly pour a very thin stream of liquid lightly over food.

Dusting:	Sprinkling lightly over surface with dry, powdery ingredients such as sugar, spices, or flour.
Fleishig:	Meat or its derivatives, or combinations containing the same; dishes and utensils so designated.
Flouring:	Dusting or rolling in flour.
Folding in:	Combining ingredients with a gentle stroke of spoon or fork downward through the mixture, along bottom of container, and then upward until blended and air is incorporated.
Grating:	Reducing to fine particles, usually with a grater or food processor.
Grease:	To lightly coat a pan with some fat to prevent foods from sticking and to help browning.
Grebenes:	See cracklings.
Kashruth:	Regulations taken from Jewish law codes pertaining to food and daily life.
Knead:	To work into a smooth and elastic mass by pressure of the hand, using the heel of the thumb.
Latkes:	Pancakes that are usually deep-fried.
Leaven:	To cause a mixture to rise while it is baking by adding baking powder, baking soda, or yeast.
Melt:	To heat until liquid and pourable.
Milchig:	Milk derivatives; foods containing no meat derivative; dishes and utensils so designated.
Mince:	To chop or cut up very fine.
Mixing:	Combining ingredients until evenly distributed.
Parboiling:	"Al dente," cooking in boiling water until partially soft.
Pare:	To remove outer covering from fruits and vegetables with a knife.
Pareve:	Neutral – can be eaten with dairy or meat meals; containing no meat derivatives and no milk derivatives.
Peel:	To strip off outer covering from fruits and vegetables; the outer skin or rind of a fruit or vegetable.
Pesahdic:	Prepared for the week of Passover; approved for Passover use and marked accordingly.
Pit:	To remove the pits from fruit.
Plump:	To soak dried fruits in liquid until they swell and are rehydrated.

Preheat:	To set oven at the desired temperature before use so that desired temperature is reached before food is put in to cook.
Render:	To liquefy solid fat over low heat.
Rind:	The outer skin or peel of a fruit or vegetable.
Sauté:	To cook until browned and tender in small amount of fat in uncovered pan.
Schmaltz:	Chicken or goose fat.
Shredding:	Cutting or tearing into thin pieces or strips, with the aid of a knife, grater, or food processor.
Sift:	To pass dry ingredients, usually flour, through a fine-mesh strainer to remove lumps and lighten texture.
Simmer:	To cook liquid alone or along with other ingredients over low heat. Some small bubbles will usually appear on the surface.
Soufflé:	A baked food, either a dessert or entree, made light and fluffy by the addition of beaten egg whites before cooking.
Steam:	To cook food covered over a small amount of boiling water.
Stir:	To blend a mixture together using a spoon in a circular motion.
Stock:	Broth made from meat, poultry, fish, or vegetables with the addition of herbs and spices.
Whipping:	Using a brisk, rotary motion to allow air into mixture of ingredients; beating eggs, cream, or combinations of both with fork or rotary beater.

INDEX

FAVORITE RECIPES

Name   Page #

_____

_____

_____

_____

_____

_____

_____

_____

_____

_____

_____

_____

_____

_____

_____

_____

_____

_____

NOTES

ABOUT THE AUTHOR

Her
egg shaped
face is crowned
with golden ringlets of golden noodles.

She has lemon shaped eyes, dark as luscious blueberries.

When she laughs almond
Tears pass her plump, rosy
cheeks to cherry red lips.

Her complexion is smooth
as milk and honey.

Nina has a cute little nose with
raisin shaped nostrils to savor the aroma of kugel baking.

Ears resembling apple halves hear rave reviews from fans.

With a personality as sweet as sugar,
she is a peach of a gal and her friends
are just nuts about her.

She is quite shy and modest!

Events and celebrations catered by Nina Yellin always feature kugel. Her extensive collection of kugel recipes, experimentation, testing, and research make her a leading kugel authority. Throughout her adult life and during extensive travel she has studied and mastered the art of Jewish cooking. She is a member of PMA and the American Institute of Wine and Food.

KUGEL, KNISHES, AND OTHER TASTY DISHES

A cookbook is always appreciated and shows thoughtfulness on the part of the presenter. Consider buying several for relatives and friends. Especially nice as a hostess gift or for bridal showers, cookbooks are also welcomed for holidays, birthdays, and anniversaries.

Does your organization need a fund raiser? Write to the address below for details.

Please send_____copies of
Kugel, Knishes, and Other Tasty Dishes

Enclosed is $18.95 per book plus $2.50 shipping and handling for 1-6 books. For priority mail, add 4.00 for 1 or 2 books; for each additional book add $1.00.

Total amount enclosed $_____.

Make check or money order payable to:

Smylan Reed Books
P. O. Box 271314
Flower Mound, TX 75027-1314

Credit Card #_____Mastercard ___Visa___

Name on account_____Expiration date_____

Please Print:

Name: _____

Address: Street _____Apt. #_____

City_____ State_____ Zip_____

Phone # (_____)_____e-mail address_____